-6

Managing Leisure

Byron Grainger-Jones

OXFORD   AUCKLAND   JOHANNESBURG   MELBOURNE   NEW DELHI

Butterworth-Heinemann
Linacre House, Jordan Hill, Oxford OX2 8DP
225 Wildwood Avenue, Woburn MA 01801-2041
A division of Reed Educational and Professional Publishing Ltd

A member of the Reed Elsevier plc group

First published 1999
Transferred to digital printing 2001

British Library Cataloguing in Publication Data
Grainger-Jones, Byron
   Managing leisure
   1. Leisure industry – management
   I. Title
   338.4'791'068

ISBN 0 7506 3717 X

Printed in Great Britain by Antony Rowe Ltd, Eastbourne

PLANT A TREE
British Trust for Conservation Volunteers

FOR EVERY TITLE THAT WE PUBLISH, BUTTERWORTH-HEINEMANN
WILL PAY FOR BTCV TO PLANT AND CARE FOR A TREE.

www.bh.com

Contents

Preface

Although this book was conceived while I worked at Guildford, and researched while I worked at Southampton, it was written entirely outside the United Kingdom, partly in France but mostly in Spain.

My unexpectedly peripatetic lifestyle made the exercise somewhat fraught but gave me a feeling that I should try to avoid the parochialism which is common in other leisure management texts and which implies that the United Kingdom represents the extent of the known universe.

But I also saw that some topic areas were inescapably unique to the UK, for example the subsidy system, the regulatory environment and the National Lottery. Similarly the descriptive component which comprises the bulk of the first chapter is unavoidably UK oriented. Nevertheless, much of the book is concerned with the practice of leisure management and not with the theory – though theory is mentioned where necessary. The chapter headings, too, suggest that the emphasis is on the active verb 'managing' and not on the abstract noun 'management'.

The book's primary readership is anticipated to be undergraduate and HND students undertaking leisure courses at institutions of higher education. Probably the majority will be based in the UK, but unlike their predecessors, will contemplate working in countries other than their own.

The secondary readership – second in terms of number but certainly not in terms of importance – is the leisure management profession itself. In my experience, very few managers have the time, or perhaps inclination, to read whole books on the discipline, but keep themselves up to date through conferences, briefings, newsletters and so forth. In order that they may be tempted by the 'practical' emphasis of this book, I have endeavoured to keep each chapter as self-contained as possible.

Those studying allied vocational subjects at degree or HND level, such as tourism, arts administration or hotel management, may also find parts of the book relevant to their own studies, and may thus constitute the third readership. Tourism in particular is such an enormous industry – probably the largest in the world – that its connections with the leisure industry (which is massive too) deserve greater recognition.

The fourth category of readers may be members of the public who have their own reasons for learning something of the leisure industry – perhaps they contemplate taking up a new activity, or establishing a commercial 'leisure venture', or making a career move from their current job to one within the industry.

Above all, I trust that my own enthusiasm for a 'positive approach' – to life generally and to leisure specifically – is manifest from the text. That I have been fortunate in my management experience, in my academic work and in my leisure activity is not the only explanation, for I have tried always to 'make things happen' – and that is essentially what this book is recommending.

Byron Grainger-Jones
Universidad de Alicante
Campus de San Vicente
Alicante, Spain

Acknowledgements

My thanks are due to many people, friends and former colleagues mostly, but the following deserve especial mention:

Dr David Ball, Director, RAMA
Francine Beaudoin, Rouen, France
Colin Billyard, freelance musician, formerly Team Co-ordinator, Guildford College of Further and Higher Education
Christine Brockman, Head of Creative Studies, Guildford College of Further and Higher Education
Anthony Clift, consultant, formerly Borough Engineer and Surveyor, Elmbridge Borough Council, Esher, Surrey
Laurence Embury, Director of Housing, Northampton Borough Council
Edward Grayson QC (author, *Sport and the Law*)
Ian Hamilton, Director, Hamilton Patrick Associates, Thetford
Ian Henry, University of Loughborough
Guy Holmes, Senior Lecturer, Southampton Institute of Higher Education
Institute of Leisure and Amenity Management (ILAM)
Bob Laventure, Field Liaison Manager, Physical Activity Project, Health Education Authority, London
Adrian Lee, Head of Studies, IMIAS, University of Alicante
Jose Mateo Martinez, Director, IMIAS, University of Alicante
Migdalia Mouzo, University of Alicante
Rob Phillips, Training Officer, Thorpe Park, Surrey
Douglas Stewart, formerly Director of Leisure Services, London Borough of Hackney
Peter Trigg, Wirral Metropolitan College
Jeff Warburn, Client Officer, Guildford Borough Council
Keith Webster, Safety and Security Manager, RFU, Twickenham
Professor Tim Wheeler, formerly Southampton Institute of Higher Education

David Williams, Training and Safety Manager, Thorpe Park, Surrey
Betty Young, formerly Head of Press, Financial Services Authority
Paul H. Young, formerly External Finance Manager, Independent Television
  Commission

Abbreviations

ACAS	Advisory Conciliation and Arbitration Service
AONB	Area of Outstanding Natural Beauty
BCU	British Canoe Union
BTCV	British Trust for Conservation Volunteers
CAP	Common Agricultural Policy (of European Union)
CCPR	Central Council of Physical Recreation
CCT	Compulsory competitive tendering
CCTV	Closed-circuit television
CIPFA	Chartered Institute of Public Finance and Accountancy
COSHH	Control of Substances Hazardous to Health (Regulations)
CPS	Crown Prosecution Service
DSO	Direct service organization
DTI	Department of Trade and Industry
EHLASS	European home and leisure accident surveillance system
EOC	Equal Opportunities Commission
HASS	Home accident surveillance system
HEA	Health Education Authority
HSE	Health and Safety Executive
ILAM	Institute of Leisure and Amenity Management
LASS	Leisure accident surveillance system
NESA	National Entertainment Safety Association
NFU	National Farmers Union
NPFA	National Playing Fields Association
OPCS	Office of Population Censuses and Surveys
PEL	Public entertainment licence
PPL	Phonographic Performance Ltd
PRS	Performing Right Society
PSBR	Public sector borrowing requirement
QUANGO	Quasi-autonomous non-governmental organization

RIDDOR	Reporting of Injuries Diseases and Dangerous Occurrences Regulations
RFU	Rugby Football Union
RoSPA	Royal Society for the Prevention of Accidents
RSPB	Royal Society for the Protection of Birds
SSSI	Site of Special Scientific Interest
VDU	Visual display unit
VPL	Video Performance Ltd
VR	Virtual reality

Introduction

Questions

At the end of this Introduction you should be able to undertake the following:

1 Identify the main differences between the three sectors of 'leisure supply', in terms of their social and financial objectives.
2 Discuss the advantages and disadvantages of expecting the private sector to supply all leisure facilities and programmes.
3 Consider how can the demand for leisure be assessed, and what may be the problems attached to each method.

Purpose of the text

The leisure industry has grown to be so substantial and diverse that training is taken as axiomatic. As recently as 30 years ago, however, there were no 'leisure management' higher education courses in the United Kingdom but only courses in physical education. At the time of writing, there are approximately 65 institutions offering degrees and Higher National Diplomas in leisure management. This is in itself a remarkable testimony to a discipline which, like tourism management, has developed rapidly in the post-war period.

Similarly, degree courses in leisure management are widely available at American Universities, as are opportunities for research in the discipline.

There will inevitably be those who adopt a purist approach, arguing that such courses are 'vocational' and not 'academic'.

On this basis, leisure management would not be perceived as a 'discipline'. The general acceptance of vocational subjects as being worthy of university attention has changed this way of thinking, except perhaps at the more elitist institutions.

The real world presses on notwithstanding: the reality is that people need to be trained for a growing labour market, and universities themselves need money to sustain their own existence.

That said, vocational degrees do present problems, in that the division between theory and practice is not hard and fast. There is of course a 'heritage' to this subject, in the form of social history – and there are increasingly laid down modes of operation, in the form of rules and regulations. There is also a massive industry (on the 'supply' side of the equation) and a huge number of customers (on the 'demand' side).

Inevitably, therefore, degree/HND courses in leisure management will look to a labour market which has specific characteristics and needs. Whatever the universities think, the industry expects the holders of such qualifications to be potential managers and not just academic theorists. If skill is taken to be the application of knowledge, then management is a synthesis of both, i.e. knowing when and how to make decisions.

This book is aimed at those students who have decided to embark upon such a course. It is not meant to be encyclopaedic, nor prescriptive, but merely to indicate some general principles as the basis for understanding the subject as a whole and for making management decisions in the future.

Chapter 1 examines the 'social context' within which the discipline must operate. An industry which is both demand- and supply-led must inevitably be sensitive to the vagaries of each phenomenon.

Changes to the nature of the family and to the nature of work have had a substantial effect upon the demand for leisure. Likewise, the acceptance of 'consumer choice' as a general principle has meant that greater diversification is anticipated. As a corollary, demographic change (in western Europe at least) means that an increasingly elderly society has more 'disposable time', and possibly more 'disposable income' to commit to leisure.

Technology, in the meantime, continues to move at an astonishing pace. The opportunities for 'home-based' leisure are growing exponentially, into realms previously undreamt of – truly into dreams themselves, with the advent of virtual reality. For many people, television (even in the days before colour) has already become a form of reality that dominates their leisure time. Who is to say what the future will hold? We need at least some framework to put the technology into a social context, whilst recognizing (in the Marxist sense) that society always lags behind the technology.

Chapter 2 examines the whole area of 'constraint'. As the leisure industry has grown so large and diverse, there has been a need for control (over safety) and regulation (over standards). Simultaneously, there has been a growth in leisure-related accidents leading to litigation, and some of these accidents have involved large numbers of people. The chapter goes on to describe some fundamental legal principles which relate to leisure management in the United Kingdom, whilst recognizing that the actual laws may not be the same in other countries.

Chapters 3, 4 and 5 consider aspects of management which are actually quite distinct, but are often confused since one manager will frequently be responsible for all of them. The management of physical resources (land, water, buildings, plant and equipment) is itself a very substantial job, as any estate manager will confirm. Add to that the management of people (staff, customers, contractors), and one sees a very complex set of responsibilities. And then there is money – yet another area where knowledge is often presupposed, rather than properly explained. Present-day managers are expected to be familiar with the basic principles of accounting, with business plans and with the methodology of budgetary monitoring. Some, indeed, will be expected to prepare not only budgets but also trading and profit and loss accounts.

Chapter 6 establishes some principles and guidelines for the management of programmes or events, a distinct area from previous chapters, although previously considered aspects do come into the frame.

Chapter 7 is about the management of risk. A great deal of leisure management is concerned with risk, in one way or another, and therefore the subject is addressed in some detail. To an extent, this chapter can be taken together with Chapter 2, except that the regulatory context is embedded in the legal and moral frameworks of western European and North American societies, whereas 'risk management', at different levels, is common throughout the world.

Chapter 8 presents an analysis of the leisure manager's role in the light of preceding chapters and also provides some guidance on securing a job within the industry.

Finally, students are expected to make use of the reading list which is provided at the end of each chapter. They may also wish to follow up some of the references which are mentioned. In the author's experience, 'reading for pleasure' is not something which students readily appreciate, largely because textbooks are often dull and in any case such reading is perceived as being 'forced upon' the reader, and not willingly chosen. My hope is that the first reservation may be disproved, and that thereby the second will be overlooked.

Before we take a look at the leisure industry in some detail, something should be said about the definition of 'leisure' itself.

Defining 'leisure'

Defining 'leisure' is surprisingly difficult – it is one of those words which is used often, like 'society' or 'community', but has no precise meaning. Often, indeed, it is defined by its context in a book, paragraph or sentence, and underlain by assumptions about value.

Take one simple example: we have 'tourists', defined for the most part as 'people who partake of leisure away from home'; but we do not talk of 'leisure-ists'. Connotations attached to the word 'leisure' have also changed over time.

Leisure is sometimes described in one of four modes:

1   Leisure as time. There is a danger of saying that 'leisure is whatever occupies my leisure time', which being a tautology leads nowhere. None the less, it is poss-ible to identify 'disposable time', just as one may identify 'disposable income'. But is disposable time the same as leisure time? Surely some further attribute is required to make leisure time something distinct from disposable time?

2   Leisure as expenditure. The statement that 'leisure is whatever absorbs my leisure spend' is also tautological, but makes it clear that choice or 'disposable' monies are involved. Food must be bought, as must clothing, warmth, shelter. The finance that is left over from these necessities can be spent as one wishes, and is thus regarded as 'disposable'. One problem here is defining exactly what constitutes a necessity as opposed to a luxury. Telephones, vacuum clean-ers, fridges, microwaves, cookers, televisions – all were considered luxuries when they were first introduced onto the market, but are now essential com-ponents of modern life. Expenditure on labour-saving devices (sometimes called 'white goods') may not constitute a leisure spend per se, though the devices do create the possibility of additional leisure time.

3   Leisure as a state of being. If leisure is a condition, or state of being, then it is equally fuzzy as a concept. Such a description – or definition – would suggest that leisure is whatever one considers to be leisure, acknowledged perhaps in retrospect.

Individuals perceive things differently at various moments, according to their moods – and states of enjoyment vary from person to person. One person may receive as much pleasure from watching a soap opera on television as another would derive from watching a live performance of King Lear, for example.

The saying that 'Leisure equals pleasure' also comes to mind – except that something can be 'pleasurable' but never 'leisure-able'.

4   Leisure as antithesis. Leisure is often thought of as something-which-is-not-work, or as something-which-is-not-enforced. Defining or describing some-

thing by 'what it is not' is rather unsatisfactory, since it would take a sizeable exercise in elimination to determine what it actually is.

However, in general terms, people do tend to think of leisure as the antithesis of work and of all those other chores, like shopping, cooking, etc., which are inescapable. Leisure thus becomes an 'end', and work through its earning potential, a 'means' towards that end.

Other words are either added to leisure automatically, e.g. 'leisure pursuits', or are substituted for the word 'leisure' itself. We have 'sports', 'games', 'play', 'pastimes', 'hobbies' and of course 'recreation'. For some of these, physical activity is a prerequisite (for sports, perhaps), whereas for others, it is the rules that matter (for games, for example).

Ultimately, it may be that no simple definition of leisure is adequate by itself, since the concept presupposes others. Notwithstanding, there is something to be said for 'objective measurement', and therefore a time-based definition is more acceptable than others. By this means, leisure may be defined as 'the application of disposable time to an activity which is perceived by the individual as either beneficial or enjoyable'.

The distinction between what is beneficial and what is enjoyable might appear arbitrary but is not so. Not all enjoyable activities are beneficial, nor all beneficial activities enjoyable. The word 'application' might also be misunderstood: it is not intended to be moralistic in the sense of 'dedication', but rather in the non-judgemental sense of 'time-allocation'.

Even here a problem arises. Who is to say what is beneficial and what is not? And can the participant in a pursuit really judge whether or not that pursuit is beneficial, even where it is, as far as they are concerned, relatively enjoyable? Once the definition is extended, it becomes necessary to impose more and more value judgements.

Before examining some aspects of management, we must say something about the nature of leisure supply and leisure demand, in order that the two chapters on 'context' make sense.

Leisure supply

The suppliers of leisure services are generally described as falling into three categories:

*   public sector

- private sector
- voluntary sector.

The public sector

The public sector exists where central and/or local government directly provides, or otherwise facilitates, leisure services. The words 'otherwise facilitates' are not meant to be obscure – they would encompass, for example, situations where a local authority pays a private sector operator to provide a particular leisure service. The point is that monies to run the service are derived from the public, in the form of taxation. In this sense, they are monies which are extracted, and not given willingly. And decisions about 'what money is spent on' are made by some form of collective, either democratically elected, as with a local authority, or otherwise selected, as with a sports council, countryside commission or arts council.

Like the private sector, the public sector is constrained by finance, i.e. by the income which it receives. Unlike the private sector, however, the public sector has no 'equity-holders' or shareholders, nor can it use its fixed assets (land and buildings mostly) as collateral for borrowing. Its decisions – especially regarding 'discretionary services' such as leisure – can always be challenged.

In contrast, the private sector has objectives which are far easier to understand. These are ultimately profit driven, but may additionally be related to securing a particular percentage share of a particular market. Losses may even be acceptable if in the longer term these are transformed into profits through the acquisition of a monopoly or near-monopoly.

The private sector has long been involved in the leisure industry, and indeed some parts of that industry have always been commercially oriented, such as cinemas, bingo halls, pubs, restaurants and theme parks.

The voluntary sector exists through the (largely unpaid) efforts of people within the community who wish to see a service provided either exclusively for their members or for the benefit of the community as a whole. The voluntary aspect of their operation is reflected in their legal status: they are normally Registered Charities, and receive some benefits where taxation is concerned as well as Discretionary Rate Relief granted by local authorities.

Origins

Public sector provision in the United Kingdom goes back to the nineteenth century, for the most part, when an enlightened liberal middle class became concerned at the social effects of an over-rapid urbanization, and set out to achieve the following:

- Improvements to administrative structures, e.g. by establishing the basic format of local government, on lines similar to the Poor Law Reform model, with policy made at the centre but implemented locally.
- Improvements to conditions of sanitation and hygiene, to offset the worst characteristics of over-populated urban areas, e.g. through various Public Health Acts, giving local authorities the power to provide public baths and suchlike if they so wished.
- Improved opportunities for access to learning and culture, e.g. through the provision of art galleries and museums, plus support for orchestras, such as the Bournemouth Symphony Orchestra.

Of course, less enlightened influences were also at work, for example:

- Concerns over public order meant the suppression of popular forms of recreation (boxing competitions, animal baiting, dog-fighting).
- Religious influences (which included the Society for the Suppression of Vice, revived in 1802, and the Temperance Society) played their part in attempts to protect the Sabbath, restrict gambling, and reduce the opportunities for people to drink alcohol. Similar causes gave rise to prohibition in the United States, much later.
- Concern over public order and social control: anxiety was expressed by the authorities about the potential for riots at large gatherings, whether they were political or merely recreational. The suppression of Blood Sports Act 1833 effectively banned the more working class pursuits such as dog-fighting, and shooting. Other sports were 'controlled' rather than abolished, e.g. football and boxing.

By the mid-nineteenth century, the state's role changed from one of suppressing popular recreation to one of promoting 'recreational forms'. Thus, Working Mens' Clubs, Mechanics Institutes and Literary Societies were meant to channel energies away from music halls and brothels, into more intellectual realms.

Public provision in the twentieth century

The background to local authority provision, and state involvement with sports and culture, perhaps explains how public sector involvement became so substantial in the United Kingdom. Concern over the 'fitness of the population' in the 1930s, for example, culminated in the Physical Recreation and Training Act 1937.

The same circumstances did not arise elsewhere – no other country experienced the same massive upheaval, population growth and social fragmentation brought about by the Industrial Revolution, as did the United Kingdom.

State-sponsored organizations – or QUANGOS as we now call them – became features of a post-war society which tried to improve social conditions. State intervention, by a new post-war Labour administration, in the arts, sports and countryside, meant that legislation was required which would eventually lead to the creation of new organizations. The Arts Council (1946), soon replaced the Council for Entertainment, Music and the Arts. A later Labour administration, which came to power under Harold Wilson in 1964, was to continue the process, by establishing first the Sports Council, and later the Countryside Commission, which replaced the National Parks Commission in 1968.

State intervention in cultural affairs had, in fact, seen an earlier precedent, with the establishment of the British Broadcasting Corporation (the BBC) in 1927.

At a local level, public bodies proliferated – and they in turn continued in the liberal-enlightened tradition of providing services considered to be of benefit to the community. There were, however, to be few private benefactors but only ratepayers and tax payers.

The return of market forces: 1979

The year 1979 saw the victory of a radical Conservative government, with Margaret Thatcher at its helm. Dedicated to 'rolling back the power of the state', Mrs Thatcher's government began to scrutinize many of the more 'socialist' initiatives which previous Labour administrations had instigated. There was to be a curb upon the Public Sector Borrowing Requirement (PSBR) – and since monies paid to local authorities, via the Rate Support Grant, constituted part of the PSBR, what could be more natural than a squeeze upon local government?

A rate-capping mechanism was introduced, and its effect upon public sector leisure provision was considerable. Some Conservative-led authorities saw privatization as a way out of their dilemma. After all, it was not mandatory to manage leisure facilities, nor even provide most of them in the first place. Through what is termed 'enabling legislation', local authorities are able to provide leisure centres, parks, swimming pools, entertainment venues, etc., if they wish – but they do not have to.

The Local Government Act 1988 became the instrument which was to change the relationship between public sector provision and private sector management, by forcing local authorities to seek competitive tenders for the management of their facilities, including leisure facilities.

The aftermath

The adversarial approach adopted by Mrs Thatcher's government towards local government made the relationship difficult, especially between a staunchly Conservative administration and some Labour-led local authorities. As it turned out, compulsory competitive tendering (CCT) affected sports provision more than it did provision for the arts. Libraries were unaffected by CCT, though rumours constantly swept the Library Association. Many entertainment venues, fearing the worst, used the mechanism of the Charitable Trust to avoid CCT. The Countryside Commission remained intact; the Sports Council was split and the Arts Council of Great Britain was to be replaced by four Arts Councils. Regional Arts Associations, as a result of the Wilding Report, became Regional Arts Boards. 'Fragment and Rule' seemed to be the order of the day. Whether some of the wounds will be healed by a Labour administration which came to power in 1997 remains to be seen.

What is left for local government to do? Surprisingly, and in spite of CCT, a great deal. Local authorities still spend a large sum of money on museums and galleries (approximately £150 million in 1997), for example, and an even greater sum on the maintenance of parks and open spaces (approximately £1 billion).

Leisure functions of local authorities

Local authorities remain major players in the leisure business, in the following ways:

- Ownership of land used for leisure purposes, e.g. recreation grounds, parks, play areas, where these are dedicated as public open space.
- Ownership of some land used as commons and village greens.

Subject to CCT outcomes, either 'client' role in relation to leisure land, or 'client' role plus 'maintenance' role.

- Ownership of leisure buildings, e.g. swimming pools, libraries, leisure centres, public halls, youth clubs, museums, art galleries, entertainment venues, plus some regional film theatres.
- Management of some of the above, subject to CCT outcomes, or fulfilment of 'client' role.
- Direct promotion of events (e.g. town shows), entertainment programmes (e.g. arts festivals), and sports programmes (e.g. summer holiday schemes).
- Direct provision of facilities, through capital expenditure – subject to government borrowing approval.

- Employment of managerial, administrative and clerical staff, plus specialist 'animateurs' (e.g. sports/arts development officers) as a means to undertake the functions described above.

In addition, local authorities have two other roles which affect leisure provision, namely:

- Licensing and inspection, e.g. granting of Public Entertainment Licences, inspection with regard to Food Hygiene regulations (see Chapter 2).
- Planning function, e.g. granting of outline or detailed planning consent to leisure projects, whether sought by the public, private or voluntary sector.

It should be noted that unitary authorities and county councils carry out functions related to the network of public footpaths (total of 1676 miles) and to the registration of common land.

The private sector

The cinema industry is, in many ways a microcosm of the private sector as a whole. With the exception of lottery monies granted towards film production in the United Kingdom, the cinema business has a long record of 'living off its wits': it has experienced boom times and bad times; more recently, it has diversified into completely new areas.

Cinema effectively took the place of the music hall, as a form of mass entertainment – but its impact was to be far greater. What began as a 'fairground novelty' in France, America and the United Kingdom soon grew into the most popular form of entertainment in the world, until television came along in the 1950s.

The growth of the industry was remarkable, particularly during the inter-war period (between 1918 and 1939). Liverpool contained 32 cinemas in 1913, for example, but 96 in 1939; Birmingham's cinemas increased from 57 to 110 in the same period.

By 1939, when the cinema industry was at its strongest, there were an estimated 23 million attendances each week. The fall in attendances that was to follow has seemingly been halted by the development of 'multiplexes' (and soon 'megaplexes' perhaps) often built in out-of-town sites. Greater efforts at niche marketing plus major 'blockbuster releases' have also bolstered the industry.

This brief vignette shows how one private sector industry has survived for virtually a whole century, despite the introduction of a form of entertainment which many said would 'signify the end' for the silver screen.

Due to the influence of Hollywood, we also see greater diversification by film production companies who market products associated with their films, and also the opening up of the larger film sets to become theme parks. The film *Titanic* (1998 release), for example, re-awakened interest in proposals to raise the original ship, and even the replica built for the film may well be purchased as a theme park attraction (at American Adventure World, Derbyshire) in its own right.

Private sector companies: The major operators

Private sector involvement with leisure is obviously much wider than cinema alone. The development of pubs, restaurants, wine-bars and so on has for example meant that large brewing companies have diversified from 'product manufacture and delivery', to 'service delivery' in the many thousands of eating places and bars to be found in the United Kingdom.

Diversification niche marketing and company takeovers are all very much features of the private sector leisure business. Newer players in the game are realizing that the 'secondary income', from product sales can be as significant as income derived from the main activity itself. Thus, one sees Aston Villa football club, Manchester United, Newcastle United and Tottenham Hotspur selling shares, alongside other major leisure companies such as EuroDisney, Ladbrokes, First Leisure (see Figure 0.1), Granada and the Rank Organization.

First leisure plc

- Stock market value £522 million
- Share price   318p
- Work force   5270

1/2 Year	£
Sales	£88.8m
Pre-tax profit	£17.2m
Earnings/share	7.24p
Dividend/share	2.64p

Business (by turnover)

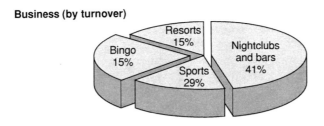

Figure 0.1 A profile of First Leisure, 1997. *Source: The Guardian*, 25 June 1997

Currently the groupings appear as follows:

- media/music/publishing
- night-clubs/resorts/bingo
- hotels/catering/entertainment
- television/film/communications
- breweries/pubs/wine-bars.

Smaller operators

At the interface with the public sector, companies have evolved which obtain much of their work from local authorities. For many years, there have been horticultural and arboricultural (i.e. tree specialist) firms which operated in this way. As a result of CCT, introduced in 1988, leisure management companies sprang up with very little pedigree, and fewer assets. Being asset-poor, their collateral was to be the 'total of contracts held', and not tangible assets such as land or buildings. Some struggled to compete within the strange new environment, and one company went bankrupt.

In the meantime, fitness centres grew more popular – whereas bingo became less so – and larger operators (such as First Leisure) began to take an interest in acquiring the former.

Smaller private sector companies may therefore be categorized as follows:

- specialist sports provision by key individuals, often former internationals, e.g. some indoor tennis centres in the United Kingdom, and some fitness centres
- small-scale operations to provide night-clubs, bars, cafés, restaurants
- small-scale operations to provide 'games' (not necessarily gambling) venues, e.g. laser game centres
- horticultural/arboricultural maintenance-based companies
- leisure management companies, operating centres owned by local authorities
- private sector museums and art galleries
- sports promotions companies (to organize events or to 'sell' the presence of famous sports personalities)
- promoters/artists' agents, e.g. Psycho Management
- various private sector companies who derive much of their income from the demand for leisure, e.g. coach companies, travel operators, video hire shops, television rental firms, sportswear shops, etc.

The private sector is probably stronger than ever, through careful selection of activity areas, and by the judicious accumulation of physical assets (land, buildings, equipment). Since unwise entry into an untried market can lead to financial ruin, the private sector tends to 'play safe' by waiting to see how things go (with leisure management firms, perhaps?) before committing itself. Involvement with more populist forms of activity – cinemas, ten-pin bowls, bars, fast-food, casinos – is seen as the hallmark of the private sector.

The voluntary sector

The voluntary sector is often under-estimated in its scale and significance. Unlike the public sector, it tends to provide facilities and services for its own devotees and unlike much of the private sector has no shares to sell, though it is itself a large purchaser of goods and services.

Examples of groups within the voluntary sector are as follows:

- amateur dramatic societies
- photographic clubs
- art societies
- choral societies
- hockey clubs
- cricket clubs
- tennis clubs
- civic societies
- conservation groups
- local history societies.

Many clubs and societies have a long history, and are proud of their record. Sports clubs have a distinct advantage in this respect, since they can point to shields, medallions and trophies all won by past members or by their teams. Non-sports clubs and societies tend to live more 'in the present and the future', looking forward to the next production or the next project.

The voluntary sector has had to struggle in order to survive. Investment in land and/or buildings is sometimes supplemented by grant aid (from local authorities or from sports/arts bodies) but frequently requires a financial commitment from members themselves.

Some clubs, especially for cricket, tennis and rugby, have had the good fortune to be blessed with members who have professional expertise in the property sector, and have thus been able to secure their freeholds; others, being less fortunate in that respect, end up leasing their facilities (often from a local authority) or merely renting rooms in a church hall or community centre in order to hold their meetings.

That said, some sports clubs have been granted leases which are as good as freeholds: one hockey club occupying a large site near Kingston-upon-Thames has a 999-year lease granted by its local authority.

Depending very much on the goodwill of its members, and the generosity of local government, the voluntary sector adds a great deal to community life in the United Kingdom, and not only at 'local level'. Many national organizations, such as the National Playing Fields Association, the British Trust for Conservation Volunteers, and various National Federations (e.g. of music societies) add their weight to protest at any moves by central government (e.g. in taxation matters) which might affect their constituent groups and individual participants.

National bodies involved in United Kingdom leisure

National bodies involved in the different forms of leisure in the United Kingdom are identified below. They are QUANGOs for the most part, deriving all or most of their funds from central government.

Arts/museums

- Arts Councils for England, Wales, Scotland, Northern Ireland
- Foundation for Sport and the Arts
- Association for Business Sponsorship of the Arts
- National Federation of Music Societies
- Museum and Galleries Commission
- The Museums Association

Film

- British Film Institute
- Scottish Film Council
- British Film Commission
- Children's Film and Television Foundation
- British Screen Finance (a private sector company)

Crafts/design

- The Crafts Council
- The Design Council
- Contemporary Applied Arts
- Craftworks (an independent development agency for Northern Ireland)

Sport

- Sports Councils (United Kingdom Sports Council and English Sports Council – replaced the once-unified Sports Council in 1996)
- Foundation for Sport and the Arts
- National Coaching Foundation
- Central Council of Physical Recreation
- Women's Sports Foundation
- British Olympic Association
- British Sports Association for the Disabled
- United Kingdom Sports Association for People with Learning Disability
- British Paralympic Association
- Riding for the Disabled Association
- National Playing Fields Association
- various governing bodies of sport, too numerous to mention individually

Libraries and publishing

- The Library Association
- The Publishers Association
- The Welsh Book Council
- The Book Trust

Exporting and importing 'culture'

- The British Council

Organizations involved with 'rural leisure and countryside issues' are listed in Chapter 3.

Leisure demand

The demand for leisure goods and services does indeed have certain characteristics, as follows:

- Leisure demand does not necessarily 'transfer' to other goods or services of similar cost, if the initial demand is unmet. If I cannot go for a swim, because the local pool is closed for repairs, I either have to travel a distance to find another pool, or I take some other form of exercise or I stay at home.
- Leisure demand is often seasonal, as at outdoor sports venues, but also at theatres and concert halls. Most leisure operations exhibit some seasonality, and this must be anticipated, along with the cash-flow problems it causes.
- Some forms of leisure demand are also cyclical: ten-pin bowling, for example, made its commercial appearance when many cinemas closed in the 1960s. After a decade or so, the demand reduced somewhat, only to return in a slightly different form (greater family-orientation) in the 1980s.
- External events can have a significant influence on leisure demand, e.g. during the Wimbledon fortnight sales of tennis racquets and membership applications to Tennis Clubs increase; during the Olympic Games, athletics experiences a similar surge in popularity, as does the game of football during the World Cup.
- Leisure demand has become increasingly articulated or expressed, along with a greater fragmentation into specialist activities visible through the enormous number of leisure/sport magazines which are available in the late 1990s, but were not so in the 1970s.
- Leisure demand can also be fickle, and a scare over public safety or public health can instantly reduce the number of customers to a venue. On the positive side, some leisure activities become popular very rapidly, usually as a result of television exposure, e.g. darts and snooker in the 1980s.
- Leisure demand relates to customers who are extremely diverse, unlike most retail outlets which can have clear expectations about their customers. The very unpredictability of leisure customers also causes problems: they do not have to come in the first place; if they do come, they may spend nothing except for the admission charge; if they are dissatisfied, they may say nothing, but they may not return (see Chapter 4 for more on managing customers).

All in all, leisure customers are as varied in their needs as the industry which makes available the supply of goods and services. Whether these resources are supply- or demand-led also varies. The concept of latent demand is sometimes used to describe a 'potential' which lies dormant until activated by the provision of a particular supply.

The influence of price

The proposition that demand can be secured or increased by keeping prices low has had a marked effect upon leisure provision in the United Kingdom, and the existence of a public sector (using taxpayers' monies) made such a policy possible in the past. The introduction of market forces into the scenario, during the 1980s, made such subsidies less acceptable since many were 'implicit' (i.e. buried within the local authority's accounts) or simply nonsensical. Subsidy still exists, of course, and is a subject worthy of a brief explanation.

Subsidy and leisure

One of the most baffling aspects of leisure provision in the United Kingdom is the application of subsidy. To see why subsidy (e.g. for swimming pools) came into being, one has to look at the social history of the nineteenth century. Precisely how the mechanism operates is another matter, since the bodies which operate within the machinery are often non-elected. Extensive use is made of quangos, operating on the 'arms length' principle that government makes available the money, but leaves the specialist decision making to disinterested experts.

If subsidy represents the money spent by the collective – either the taxpayers in general or Council Tax payers in particular – upon individuals or groups, then someone somewhere has to make that decision, to determine the level of subsidy (100 per cent down to 1 per cent), and on occasions to explain the rationale behind the subsidy to those who pay the taxes.

In the labyrinthine realms of local government so many subsidies are tucked away and difficult to assess. Undoubtedly CCT has made subsidy for outdoor sport – which involves substantial expenditure on grounds maintenance – far more explicit, whereas previously the figures were buried within 'revenue estimates, grounds maintenance' accounts, howsoever titled.

Subsidies towards the arts have usually been more transparent: sometimes they are in the form of grant aid (to local orchestras, say) and sometimes as revenue support towards whole facilities, such as entertainment venues. Many local authorities contribute to their respective Regional Arts Boards, and some to district arts associations that operate within their boundaries.

The subsidy machine

A diagram of the 'subsidy mechanism' is probably easier to understand than a verbal description, and Figure 0.2 represents a simplistic model which shows how money firstly moves upwards, like warm air, and then reaches the cold hands of

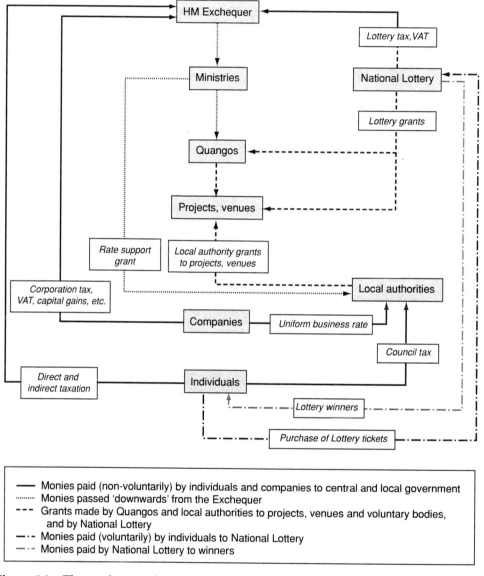

Figure 0.2   The mechanism for 'leisure subsidy' in the UK

the Exchequer – at which point it 'condenses' and cascades down. Most of the money returns to the ground, like rain, but some simply evaporates within the confines of the mechanism. (In reality it is absorbed by the running costs associated with constituent parts of the machine.)

Money is extracted from individuals and organizations in the form of taxation, both direct and indirect; it is then gathered into the Exchequer, which, after Parliamentary debate on government expenditure plans and 'the budget', allocates money to different Ministries or Departments of State.

From there, money is passed to various national quangos and ultimately to the 'final recipients'.

The National Lottery is included in the diagram not only to show a complete picture but because the money derived from the lottery has become a significant form of grant aid in the United Kingdom, especially to the voluntary sector. Government itself also receives money from the lottery, via a levy (12 per cent) on each ticket sold.

Local authorities and subsidies for sport

The Audit Commission, in advance of the introduction of CCT, carried out an interesting study, which showed amongst other things that the beneficiaries of many sports subsidies – relating mostly to leisure centres – were in fact middle class and middle income. In other words, 'social targeting' – if this was the purpose of the subsidy – appeared not to be working.

The report, entitled 'Sport for Whom? Clarifying the Local Authority Role in Sport and Recreation', made a series of recommendations, one of which was that the authorities should consider 'the extent to which support for different activities or types of facility contributes to social objectives and whether the private sector can be depended on to offer them at a price which most people can afford' (Para. 62).

A strategy review was also recommended by the report, with local authorities making conscious decisions about policy. On the matter of subsidy, the report said that 'many facilities will continue to need subsidy. This does not absolve authorities from setting financial objectives for their services ... [they] need to be sure that any subsidies are achieving their intended objective. Authorities are quite entitled to include frequent users from among the better off among [sic] those they subsidise ... the Commission believes, however, that if done, this should be a conscious decision' (Para. 65).

Figure 0.2 also shows that central government assists local authorities, through the Rate Support Grant, and this in turn makes up a sizeable proportion of their income. Local authorities also derive income from other sources, such as the Council Tax, fees and charges, rental income, etc. If it so wishes, a percentage of the total income can be spent on leisure services, but since virtually all these services are 'discretionary' and not 'mandatory', the decision rests with the respective authority. Unlike other European countries such as France and Spain, very little real autonomy is granted to local authorities in the United Kingdom. However, once a limited measure of self-government is introduced via a Scottish Parliament and Welsh Assembly, the situation will change, and a realignment of the subsidy machine will become necessary.

Subsidy and the private sector

One common misconception about subsidy needs to be cleared up. Many people believe that once a facility is handed over to the private sector, then public subsidy is no longer required.

Through the application first of CCT and then Best Value, operational deficits were supposed to be reduced, with a fixed-price contract put in place of an open-ended arrangement. But the subsidy may still be paid over where an operating deficit remains, this time to a private sector company (and its shareholders) rather than to a public authority. Whilst this may appear a perverse, undemocratic and complex system there is an argument that the private sector operates to a higher degree of efficiency, i.e. using its capital to good effect, and that therefore subsidies will become less significant as time goes by (that too was the argument for rail privatization in the United Kingdom but hardly anyone believed it then or subsequently).

Of course, the private sector benefits from the public sector in other (more legitimate) ways. Local authorities are major clients for many private contractors, ranging from grounds maintenance companies to marketing and publicity firms. Leisure facilities, as we shall see in Chapter 2 with regard to contracts, have recourse to a massive array of contracted services.

Having said all of this, it remains the case that the very idea of subsidy still rankles in some parts of the private sector, which feels that the public sector can 'undercut' them by virtue of the subsidy. That, after all, is one effect of subsidy, i.e. the reduction of admission charges, possibly to zero.

Advantages and disadvantages of subsidy

Lest it be thought that subsidy is fundamentally evil as some would have us accept, a more balanced view needs to be considered before we leave the subject.

- Social arguments for subsidy:
  1 Lower prices may help to attract poorer sections of the community, thus promoting greater equality.
  2 The community benefits by being provided with a greater range of leisure facilities than might otherwise be available.
  3 Services which are free-at-the-point-of-delivery also help to create a civilized, healthy, cultured and knowledgeable society, through schools, museums, art galleries, libraries, etc.
  4 Capital investment in deprived areas would generally not be contemplated by the private sector, unless some degree of subsidy was forthcoming.
- Economic arguments for subsidy:
  1 Price reduction should in theory increase demand, and therefore encourage greater throughput. Net income may even increase, due to the increase in throughput and a rise in secondary income (sales, of food, drinks, etc.).
  2 At a macro-economic level, subsidy may help to stimulate demand generally (for leisure goods and products), thereby benefiting all three sectors (public, private, voluntary).
- Social arguments against subsidy:
  1 Subsidy tends to gravitate towards services used by the better-off, thereby making poor people even worse off through having to pay increased taxes (see previous reference to Audit Commission Report).
  2 By subsiding 'high culture', such bodies as arts councils and regional arts boards are perpetuating class divisions based on culture – whereas they should be supporting a more democratic view of culture, i.e. 'cultural democracy' rather than the 'democratization of culture'.
  3 People do not ascribe 'value' to something which is cheap/free, but only goods or services for which they pay the 'full price'.
- Economic arguments against subsidy:
  1 The involvement of a third party, between supply and demand, reduces the efficiency of the first and the effectiveness of the second.
  2 Subsidy creates unfair competition in the market place, e.g. regional film theatres under-pricing commercial cinemas.
  3 At the micro-economic level, subsidy distorts demand through creating lower prices than the market could otherwise bear, thus making it difficult to assess 'true demand'.
  4 At a macro-economic level, the state has to extract taxation on a large scale, to pay for all the subsidies: better perhaps to charge 'true prices' (i.e. the market cost), levy less in personal taxation and let people make the choice?

The arguments for and against subsidy are expressed in a naive way, and are not intended to sway the reader in either direction. Indeed, there are those who say that the real compromise is to adopt a 'longer' standpoint, arguing that public subsidy creates a demand (and meets it by supply) to a critical point where it is large enough to justify the involvement of the private sector.

Assessing demand

The demand for leisure is more difficult to assess than its supply and there are innumerable price as well as non-price factors which will change the demand, either increasing or diminishing it. Sometimes, economists use the idea of 'latent demand' to describe a potential that is eventually translated into hard cash (purchases) once a supply has appeared.

We have already mentioned that in leisure – unlike tourism – prices have been influenced by the application of subsidy, to sustain pricing policies that ignored true 'market costs', simply because any deficits were met by the collective taxpayer or ratepayer. Be that as it may, the availability of disposable income is clearly a major determinant of demand – but other influences can also be significant, namely:

- age
- gender/sexual orientation
- education
- family life cycle
- household size
- peer group pressure
- personality type
- culture/religion
- geographical/social location
- availability of leisure time
- socio-economic position
- physiological condition
- skill and ability
- mobility, and proximity (to facilities)
- leisure perceptions (i.e. ideas about what leisure represents)
- media influences, heroes and heroines.

Each of the foregoing has its significance, according to the context in which an individual finds himself or herself. Some are described as 'constraints' by certain theorists, though what may be a constraint at one moment of life (gender for example) may be the opposite at another.

Thus the factors are neutral in themselves, and have a positive or negative effect according to the participant's own assessment. An observer of leisure participation will also have a view on the relative significance of the various factors and will inevitably impose value judgements on the interviewee's responses, however carefully any qualitative research is carried out.

For example, a teenager will be more influenced by peer group pressure and media stereotyping than will an older person. Whether these influences are to be categorized 'good' or 'bad' depends on the output: if health education programmes make people aware of the need for more exercise, then the output will be seen as positive; if media personalities are seen to be indolent and unfit, then the consequences will turn out to be negative.

Measuring the relative significance between one factor and another is not easy, simply because the 'push–pull' consequences vary over a person's life. To assess the various influences one would need to carry out qualitative surveys over an extended period of time. Alternatively, use may be made of psycho-graphic data which classifies people into specific 'lifestyles'. The cluster of 'purchasing characteristics', work habits, newspaper reading, holiday-taking and so forth is designed to identify key correlations – which may then be exploited through what is sometimes termed 'niche marketing'.

Methods of demand assessment

Various methods are used for assessing demand, depending upon the quality and quantity of what is proposed. Where a clear correlation exists between a particular leisure activity and the above-mentioned determinants, research can proceed to see in what measure they are present. This type of approach would be used prior to the construction of an indoor tennis centre by a private entrepreneur for example, since age, socio-economic status and time availability are all extremely important factors which determine whether or not the centre will be successful.

The top-down approach

One way to assess demand in a particular locality – or in the larger context for that matter – is to use the 'national standards' approach, which being based on national surveys is very much 'top-down'. This methodology argues that if, say,

there is a national standard of X swimming pools per Y thousand population, then all one has to do is divide a town's population by Y to determine how many swimming pools are needed.

National standards were used extensively by planners in the past, e.g. in the United Kingdom's first and second generation New Towns (Telford, Milton Keynes, Bracknell, Warrington, etc.). Politicians were also known to use them to argue the case for rectifying a perceived deficiency, whether for public open space, swimming pools, golf courses, public libraries or squash courts.

The standard for squash illustrates one problem with national standards, which is that many have now become dated. As the demand for squash has dropped since its boom of the 1970s, so the standard needs to be modified if it is to be credible.

Veal (1994) identifies other problems in relation to national standards, but there is no doubt that many were useful in their time, notably where sceptical local authorities were being persuaded to provide substantial sums of money for leisure centres and swimming pools.

Other top-down methods to assess demand are described by Veal as:

- The grid approach – where one grid contains a basic level of provision (a small play area say) and a quantum of grids generates the case for larger local facilities and eventually for a town centre (very much the rationale for Milton Keynes New Town)
- The hierarchical approach – where a 'hierarchy of resources' is established, per population catchment, largely in relation to sporting and entertainment needs but also in terms of community centres.

The bottom-up approach

Because the top-down approach has been somewhat discredited, an alternative has been to use research skills (sample surveys mostly) in the community itself, to ascertain what people actually wish to see by way of leisure facilities. The approach can be summarized as:

- The organic approach – waiting to see what evolves, who takes initiatives and so on
- The community development approach – where animateurs (for sports and/ or arts) work within a particular community, and by so doing generate demand. (This was the approach used in several New Towns such as Telford and Corby.)

Other methods of demand assessment

The demand for leisure goods may be assessed by quite different means: any product which appears in the market place will either secure a niche or not, depending upon price and non-price factors referred to earlier.

Leisure spending in the United Kingdom is generally estimated to be between £110 billion (ILAM, 1995) and £141 billion (Leisure Consultants, 1996). Indeed the latter company suggests that leisure spending as a percentage of all consumer spending has risen steadily from some 25.5 per cent in 1990 to 27.2 per cent in 1996. Amazing as it seems, almost as much is now spent by the average United Kingdom citizen on leisure as on housing and accommodation!

Conclusions

The leisure industry is one of the largest in the United Kingdom. It is also a major employer, with some three and a half million employees (ILAM, 1995). All household surveys show that the leisure spend is highly significant, even for poorer families (paradoxically, the spending on the National Lottery as a percentage of disposable income appears to be greater for poorer households – see Figure 0.3).

The supply side of the equation is more diverse than ever, and new opportunities for a novel experience appear all the while: a theme park is proposed; the mine shuts and becomes a museum; more sports coverage appears on more TV sports channels; a new night-club opens; the local pub now includes a restaurant ... and so on.

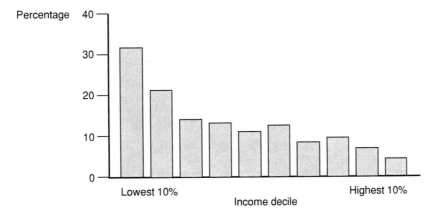

Figure 0.3 Lottery expenditure as percentage of all leisure spending, by income group, 1995. *Source: National Lottery Yearbook* (1977)

Meanwhile, back at home, the children are playing computer games, speaking to their friends, sometimes by video phone and sometimes through avatars (computer-generated models). Occasionally they watch 'real live' soccer or a Formula One race. But most of the time they prefer interactive television or VR, where they can affect the outcome.

At work, of course, things are very different – but only in a sense. Those who have a job are working more hours then ever before, due to fax machines, computers, pagers and mobile phones. Whereas several pundits argued in the 1970s that the 'leisure revolution' would bring more leisure time for everyone, in fact it appears that technology has enslaved more and more in its web, or more correctly web site.

This book tries not to adopt a sociological or even moral stance, though the author does believe that leisure time is too precious to waste on the pursuit of trivia. Instead it concentrates on the management process itself, in the belief that the leisure manager will have his or her own value judgements as to whether what is being managed is beneficial to society or not.

References and recommended reading

Barbour, S. (ed). (1997). *British Performing Arts Yearbook*. Rhinegold Publishing Ltd.

Central Office of Information. (1997). *Britain 1997: An official handbook*. The Stationery Office.

Central Statistical Office. (1994). *Social Trends. (See chapters on Leisure and on Households and Families.)*

Coalter, F. (1989). *Analysing Leisure Policy*. In I.P. Henry, *Management and Planning in the Leisure Industries*. Macmillan.

Fitzherbert, L. and Rhoades, L. (ed). (1997). *The National Lottery Yearbook and Grant-seekers' Guide*. Directory of Social Change.

General Household Survey. (1993). Office of Population Censuses and Surveys, Social Survey Division.

Gratton, C. and Taylor, P. (1991). *Government and the Economics of Sport*. Longman.

ILAM. (1995). *A Guide to the Leisure Industry – Some key facts*. Report No. 8. ILAM Information Centre.

Leisure Consultants. (1996). *Leisure Forecasts 1997–2001*. Leisure Consultants in association with Leisure Industries Research Centre.

Veal, A.J. (1994). *Leisure Policy and Planning*. Longman/ILAM Management Series.

1 The social context

Questions

At the end of this chapter you should be able to undertake the following:

1 Indicate the implications to society of an exponential growth in the technology associated with home entertainment.
2 Consider how the 'demographic shift' may affect the leisure industry of the future.
3 Discuss how changes to the nature of work may have affected attitudes to leisure.

Introduction

Like all other industries, the leisure industry is constantly adapting, sometimes in relation to internal changes but more often in relation to shifts in the external environment.

Arguably, the existence of subsidy has dampened somewhat the response rate of public sector leisure services, despite the introduction of CCT thrusting them firmly into a more competitive market place.

The commercial sector has changed both quantitatively and qualitatively (whereas the public sector still does roughly the same things that it did previously) though identifying niche markets and through exploiting links between different leisure demands.

The voluntary sector – always less vocal and less visible – continues to play an important role, often with social as well as arts/sports significance. The introduction of the National Lottery has also been of considerable benefit to many voluntary groups and organizations.

The purpose of this chapter is to identify some aspects of social change and to consider how the supply-side may respond. As we have said previously, the idea of latent demand is a useful concept, especially where home-based leisure goods are concerned – indeed, subject to price acceptability, the latent demand for such items appears to be limitless.

We examine six topics, as follows:

- choice and the leisure consumer
- the implications of demographic change
- changes to the nature of work
- home-based versus social leisure
- sport as entertainment
- theme parks.

This part of the text is not intended to act as a sociological reader, but rather to provide some thoughts by way of context. And as the social setting changes, so the regulations grow more onerous, as we shall see in the next chapter. Taken together, these two 'contextual chapters' may be considered as two sides of the same coin, the one expansive and the other restrictive ...

Choice and the leisure customer

The growth of consumer choice appears to have a certain inevitability about it, and has its origins in the transition from a feudal to what might be termed a bourgeois society. The relationship between individuals and the state has developed from foundations laid in the seventeenth century – but then the evident success of an early capitalist liberalism meant a denial of individualism to the majority, whose resources were simply insufficient to purchase land in order to acquire wealth.

The dominant characteristic of a Western society is sometimes referred to as 'possessive individualism', for example by Macpherson (1962), and whereas practices such as usury (charging interest on capital) are now commonplace, they were not always so – nor is usury acceptable to countries with 'command economies' or with traditional Islamic values.

Consumer choice in the West is now espoused as a 'right', not a 'privilege'. And as Western society has grown richer, so more individuals have the financial resources to pay more and more for their leisure.

The very individualism which has grown up with the market is also made possible through relatively low-cost technology, and thus the growth in resources for home-based entertainment has outstripped all others.

A choice between home-based and social leisure is not always available, but a thirst for the former has meant remarkable penetrations for home computers, mobile phones, computer games and the like. Doubtless, the choice will be further enhanced – if that is the correct word – by the advent of voice-activated computers, video-phones and VR systems.

So what has happened to the market as a whole? We can summarize the changes as follows:

- Greater availability of a diversified 'leisure supply', in all the sectors (public, private and voluntary) during the post-war period.
- Technological innovation which grows more 'interactive'. People may soon buy many of their goods without leaving home. Interacting with a screen will, ironically, mean less interaction with other human beings.
- Niche marketing that makes use of sophisticated concepts (consumer profiles) and computer technology. Those who sell goods or services recognize how much more effective is 'targeted marketing' as opposed to a random exercise.
- Product communications have also developed, in that consumers know more about what is available. One has only to look at the specialist magazines now sold to football fans, swimmers, marathon runners, collectors of antiques, computer buffs, opera lovers and so on, to realize how much information is to hand, almost to the point of 'information overload'.
- 'Consumer contracts' or 'customer charters' have also become more common, defining standards of service which the consumer may expect to receive. The consumer is given to understand that this is a 'right', and may well sue if the service is below par.
- Media diversity must also have an effect, if only through the impact of yet more advertising. The 'received orthodoxy' of early television in the United Kingdom, when millions switched on to see the Cup Final, has been replaced by a variety of channels wherein one can watch any number of individual sports. The 'shared national experience' is diminished thereby – but 'possessive individualism' once again is elevated.

The implications of demographic change

The true significance of an ageing society (see Figure 1.1) has yet to dawn upon the leisure industry, most of which is still geared to meet the demands of young

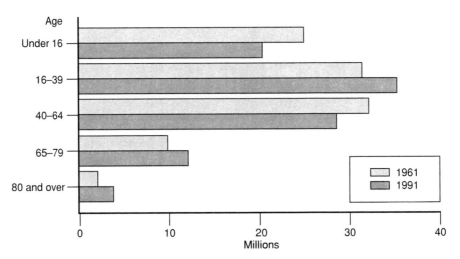

Figure 1.1   Age structure of the UK population, 1961 and 1991. *Source*: OPCS (1994)

people. By contrast, the tourist industry has realized the potential niche market which exists, and is exploiting that opportunity by way of special holidays, reduced-price long winter breaks, cruises and leisure-related breaks, e.g. for golf enthusiasts. One company, Saga, provides travel/holiday services specifically for the over-50s.

Governments have certainly begun to realize the implications of the demographic shift. The International Monetary Fund, too, reported in its biannual World Economic Outlook (April 1996) that as a result of the shift, many industrial countries will face an unsustainable bill for their pensioners.

Calling for 'generational accounting', by which today's fiscal policies are shown to affect future generations even if they do not affect current budgets, IMF economists argued that any modest reductions in youth population over the next 20 years would have but a small budgeting effect upon the costs associated with an ageing population.

Official United Kingdom government projections, made by OPCS, suggest that the number of pensioners will soar by 50 per cent in the first 30 years of the next century. By 2030, there is anticipated to be almost 80 dependants for every 100 people of working age, compared to only 63 dependants in 1991. Those aged over 75 – who require the greatest health/social services care – are expected to represent some 6 million in number by that date, compared to 3.6 million in 1991. (See Figure 1.2.)

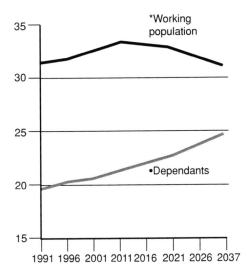

Figure 1.2   Projected working population and dependants (millions) in the UK. *Source*: OPCS Information Branch (1997)

* Population 16–64 (men)/59 (women)
• Children 0–15 plus men 65+, women 60+

OPCS attributes a temporary increase in the number of working people to a tendency for those aged 45 or over to work for longer, whereas the number of adults below the age of 30 is expected to fall from 10.8 million to only 8.9 million (*Guardian*, 3 March 1993).

Apocalyptic visions of the future are not always correct, however. If one looks at the USA, which is experiencing the same phenomenon (albeit to a lesser degree), one sees so-called 'grey power' being put to good use in the labour market (*Independent*, 9 July 1997).

We might also remind ourselves that in the USA some states are actually building 'geriatric jails'. It appears that while in 1980 there were just 9500 prisoners over the age of 55, now there are 30 000, and the figure is expected to double within 30 years (*The Sunday Times*, 13 July 1997).

Ageing and physical activity

Various researchers, such as Paffenbarger and Lee (1996) have pointed out that today's interest in sport tends to be 'vicarious' and not 'participatory': as a society, we seem more prepared to adulate the elite athletes who 'perform' for us, than to listen to the needs of our own bodies.

The above-mentioned researchers see a decline in 'vigorous occupations' as being largely to blame for a less physically active society. In addition, they see the following as contributory factors:

- mechanization
- automation
- swift communications
- rapid transport systems
- computer usage
- television viewing.

They concluded that although most of their surveys showed a public awareness that physical activity increased health and longevity, none the less actual participation rates did not reflect such awareness, with approximately 60 per cent of Americans taking little or no regular exercise.

The situation in the United Kingdom is virtually the same. In 1997, the Health Education Authority (HEA) organized a conference with the title 'Active for Later Life', in collaboration with University Department of Geriatric Medicine, Royal Free Hospital Medical School (London) and the British Geriatrics Society Special Interest Group on Health Promotion and Preventive Care. Its various reports (available from the HEA) make fascinating reading. The fact that some 30 different organizations, from countries of Europe to the USA, all participated in the conference gives some indication of widespread interest in the topic, though press coverage was not as great as it should have been.

In addition to the information from Paffenbarger and Lee's study, delegates considered the results of a study commissioned by the HEA and undertaken by Social and Community Planning Research in October 1996.

The resulting study (Finch, 1997), made 10 recommendations, as follows:

- Media images, showing only young people as fit and healthy, need to be more balanced.
- Perception of what constitutes a healthy lifestyle needs to be widened, e.g. by promoting unregimented and moderate activities such as dancing and walking.
- More information should be provided on 'safe levels of exercise'.
- The case for a healthy lifestyle should by promoted, e.g. by the media and by employers, as retirement nears.

- Activity for older males in particular needs to be promoted. (A Mintel report published in 1996 found that regular exercise was regarded as important by only 4 in 10 men, as opposed to 1 in 3 women.)
- More emphasis is needed on the non-health benefits of regular exercise, e.g. opportunities to socialize.
- Avoidance of an 'authoritarian stance', e.g. many older people shun recreation classes for fear of over-regimentation.
- More information should be delivered by the medical profession, e.g. about opportunities for fitness testing, personalized fitness programmes, exercise classes, etc.
- Facilities need to be more suitable for the older age group, both in terms of design and 'social mix' – a personalized approach by management is also seen as very important by this age group.
- People should start exercising when they are young, thus promoting the idea, at the earliest age, that physical activity is beneficial.

(A separate report by Young et al. 1997 on a similar topic was based on the Allied Dunbar National Fitness Survey, analysing data from that survey and a survey carried out by the HEA itself.)

As yet no new leisure pursuit, or sport, appears to have resulted directly from the demographic shift, which is perhaps rather strange. It may be that existing (non-contact) sports such as cricket, bowls, archery, etc. will be played until a later point in life, and that the demand for leisure activities which are less physically demanding, such as visiting museums, art galleries and historic houses, will continue to increase as the population ages.

Changes to the nature of work

If leisure is perceived as the antithesis of work or indeed work as a mechanism (means) for the achievement of leisure (ends) then it must adapt to changes in the external workplace.

Either way, that adaptation will be substantial, just as changes to patterns of work have been substantial.

Those who take a longer view are apt to argue that changes to the workplace are not as massive as might be supposed: the uncertainty faced by many workers is temporary, and is common to all workers during transitional periods, e.g. at the onset of the Industrial Revolution.

Handy (1984) mentions this idea in passing, i.e. that there have been precedents, and that the 'self-correcting cycle of adjustment' is seductive as a hypothesis – but not necessarily correct. He argues that even in the 1980s the prospects for work were changing rapidly, so that the following characteristics were becoming evident:

- A society with full employment was becoming one of part employment.
- Both 'labour' and 'manual' skills were being replaced by 'knowledge skills'.
- Traditional manufacturing industry was in decline, while service industries increased in importance.
- 'Hierarchies' and 'bureaucracies' were being replaced by looser agglomerations, represented as 'networks' and 'partnerships'.
- Rarely would a person have an 'employer for life' but rather a series of jobs or even careers.
- Increased importance attached to the 'third-age' of life, post-employment and post-family.
- Challenging of gender stereotypes, with changes to roles in the home and in the workplace.
- Work locations themselves shifting (often southwards), according to labour costs and relative exchange rates.

Many of Handy's observations have subsequently turned out to be correct. The articulation of the angst attached to such changes has however become more vociferous, particularly amongst the middle- and upper-income earners (white collars) whereas job insecurity had previously been the lot of the 'blue collars'.

The introduction of new technology and specifically IT has been blamed for much of this white collar insecurity. The idea that technology is capable of creating more jobs than it destroys is not one which necessarily reassures a person whose job is under threat, at the moment. An interesting article in *The Economist* (February 1995) poured scorn on those who predicted the 'end of work', suggesting instead that in the long run there will indeed be more jobs as a result of new technology – but that the long run can take a long time!

The effects of unemployment upon lifestyles have been well documented, but its impact upon leisure perhaps less so, with the exception of studies by Glyptis (1989).

How might the leisure industry respond to such changes? As an employer itself, there must have been some effect upon wages and salaries, notably in parts of the public sector and as a direct result of CCT. On the other hand, there appears to have been a steady increase in the number of leisure jobs available in the United

Kingdom, although many are badly paid. The fact that non-home based leisure is so labour intensive means that workers will always be required.

As a provider of services, the industry may consider the following:

- provision of more opportunities for 'belonging' (to a club or organization) through the use of databases and membership schemes
- application of more 'targeted' pricing policies, e.g. for parties of retired people, special interest groups
- operation of services on something other than a 9 a.m. to 5 p.m. basis – Thorpe Park has announced that it was to become the first of the United Kingdom's theme parks to open 24 hours a day (*Leisureweek*, April, 1995)
- removal of stereotypical constraints which remain upon certain sporting activities, e.g. mixed-gender football, hockey, cricket
- encouraging people to have a 'sport-for-life', or alternatively a series of sporting/activity pursuits, to provide continuity and personal stability (as well as much-needed exercise).

From what has been said on the subject of 'change' the reader may assume that leisure will assume a heightened significance. If one's leisure pursuits are freely chosen and freely available for most of one's life, then these become a 'refuge' or 'sanctuary', whilst everything else (work, relationships, the physical environment) changes at a bewildering pace.

It may also be argued that as work diminishes in availability (for some) and in its social content (for others, using computers to work from home), then leisure activities may represent rare opportunities for informal social interaction – perhaps indeed the only opportunities.

Home-based versus social leisure

The remarkable availability of equipment for home-based leisure is testimony to the notion of latent demand, and the United Kingdom more than many other European countries appears to adopt the various entertainment systems with an alarming rapidity. The market penetration of items such as CD players, video recorders, camcorders, computer systems has been such that very few homes indeed are totally bereft of any of the gadgetry.

Some of the systems now available have already been mentioned in the introduction, and therefore it is the implications that concern us here, and not the technology. Whereas it was once argued – by Marxist historians – that society could only respond slowly (and often badly) to changes in the nature of industry, it may now be said that society has not yet come to terms with the implications of home-based leisure systems themselves. Quite simply, it will soon be possible to use these systems to become completely isolated from the world and even to create a VR world of one's own.

An alternative is embodied in an even more alarming scenario, when television or film companies combine or cooperate with theme parks, thereby extending the non-reality even further. The 'theme park approach' to history is depressing enough, but what about when life itself is viewed as a theme park?

Assuming that leisure management is about social (and not home-based) leisure, is it possible, or appropriate, to contest the field, or should computers and VR be left to claim the ground? Can indeed the technology of home-based leisure be used to encourage social leisure, or are these completely different entities? Will the market-penetrating potential of gadgetry be such that the people end up as 'cyber-potatoes'? *The Observer* (13 July 1997) raised a question: 'will National Grid produce a generation of cyber-potatoes?', referring to the millennium project to wire up all schools and libraries in the United Kingdom to the Internet, thus connecting them to the 'information super-highway'. *The Observer* piece also made reference to another article, in *Atlantic Monthly*, on the subject of computers and schools. It appears that the article sent shockwaves through the USA's education system, where schools have been flooded with computers. The author, Todd Oppenheimer, called for a reversal of policy, in order to release the money devoted to computer hardware so that it could be spent on 'the impoverished fundamentals', i.e. the teaching of reading and numeracy, as well as on 'real experiences' to be derived from field trips.

That schools, colleges, universities and private homes are being persuaded to install so many computers is hardly surprising, but rather depressing. The computer, after all, is a remarkable tool when one has the skills and knowledge to use it properly.

And the marketing is fearsome, just as the size of the computer business is awesome. Worth $630 billion (£390 billion) in 1996, the IT industry is arguably replacing cars and housing as the driving force of the global economy. Further-more, the International Data Corporation suggested in 1997 that company spending on Net products and services will total $92 billion by the year 2000, displacing the personal computer as the engine of IT market growth. They may of course be wrong – but who is to say what nano-technology will bring along?

But trivia can be quite seductive. After all, it requires very little effort to be 'hooked'. Two examples serve to make the case: the first was that of 'television fish'

– which led eventually to 'cyber-fish'. In 1993, a new television channel in South Carolina left a camera trained on a fish tank for 14 hours a day. When the fish were eventually replaced by programmes, howls of protest arose from disgruntled viewers.

Berkeley Systems of California was to benefit from such an idea, and established its Apple Macintosh screen-saver, After Dark, which allows the operator to select from a range of fish, with the option of having sand, shells, plants and bubbles along with the simulated creatures. The registered version has more than 60 types of fish, and a built-in 'fish editor' for creating new species!

The second example of an obsession with trivia relates to the use of the Internet. In 1997, a young American woman, Jennifer Rigley, installed a small video camera in her flat, connected to a computer. The camera relays continuous images into her Internet web site, where a reported 100 million visitors from around the world look in every week (*Independent*, 26 September 1997).

The distinction between reality and fantasy thus becomes blurred – the soap opera becomes real. Indeed, who is to say what is 'real' anyway?

Sport as entertainment

Sport is not only big business, but big entertainment, to an extent that whole television channels are devoted to this single activity. The images of sport are beamed into millions of homes, and wish-fulfilment is used by sportswear manufacturers to complete the deal: wear this track suit/these running shoes/this baseball cap – and you'll be one of the stars!

There can be no doubt that media technology has totally transformed sport, turning minority sports (darts, snooker, bowls) into popular forms of entertainment, from the 1980s onwards. Sports magazines now proliferate: whereas there was one magazine for yachting enthusiasts 20 years ago, there are now 5. Every newspaper has extensive coverage of sport, and sports personalities are sought by sponsors and advertisers alike. In the meantime, football clubs go 'public', sell their 'strips' in sportswear shops, and their shares on the Stock Exchange ...

Theoretically, the greater coverage of sport should lead to more active lifestyles, if psychologists are right about role models. A temporary manipulation to buy the sportswear is, though, not sufficient. The Wall Street Analyst is quoted in *The Observer* (13 July 1997) as saying 'Eisenhower used to warn us of the military-industrial complex, but now we have a media-athletic-shoe-company-complex'. The reader can easily guess at the shoe company implicated in this scenario.

It seems likely that sport-as-entertainment will grow, rather than decline, if only for the fact that more television channels will be looking for some 'product' – and, relatively speaking, sport is a cheap alternative. Where the sport itself becomes greedy for media fees, then perhaps common sense might prevail and the media companies will refuse to pay up.

Some sports undoubtedly benefit from the media money, whereas others do not. Whether the money 'cascades down' to the young amateur players – the sportsmen and sportswomen of the future – also remains to be seen. The involvement of the Murdoch empire with the sport of Rugby Union will perhaps be a guide to what is in store ...

A theme park in every town?

The rush to develop more and more theme parks as yet sees no respite. At the time this chapter was written, for example, two such parks were announced: one at Benidorm on the Costa Blanca, and another close to Rome. In both cases, the 'theme' appears to be heritage-based. The former (Terra Mitica) promises to represent cultures from different parts of the Mediterranean littoral, and the latter the grandeur of ancient Rome. Though private backers are always sought, state or provincial governments are often expected to contribute, particularly in the development of the related infrastructure (roads, rail links, etc.).

Sometimes, the 'theme' is incidental; sometimes, indeed, there is no real theme at all, but merely a hotchpotch of rides, side shows, bars, cafes, and the rest – rather like parts of a fun-fair.

Disneyland Paris is more subtle, since the park exploits its visual connection with many Disney Corporation films. Similarly, it sells products which reinforce the connection. Eventually, as has now happened, the 'product marketing' operation becomes detached from the theme park, and operates as a free-standing retail entity in various town-centre locations.

Then again, Merrin (1998) takes her cue from the criticisms of the Disney Empire made by American writer Carl Hiassen. She concludes that the Disney version of reality as promulgated through various mechanisms – Walt Disney Pictures, Touchstone, Caravan, Miramar and Hollywood Pictures, ESPN, the Disney Channel, Arts and Entertainment, the History Channel and Lifetime, nine television stations, twenty-one radio stations, seven daily newspapers, computer software, sports franchises, and so forth – serves to diminish the human imagination by a process of 'colonization' and 'sanitization'.

Meanwhile, within the United Kingdom, established theme parks have had their measure of success, and new ones are being proposed. A scheme to build a £250 million sports and leisure park in Lancashire was announced in August 1997, by Moorfields Estates. Xanadu, as it is to be named, will include an 80 000 square feet hotel and retail complex on a 72-acre site between Liverpool and Manchester. The leisure elements are to include an 'alpine village', with ski runs and snowboarding, an aquatic centre, including a 50-metre Olympic standard pool, a leisure pool, and a 'megaplex cinema'. Those fortunate enough to live in the vicinity of Xanadu are promised a screen-based 'virtual reality experience', whatever that may be. One also reads (*Leisureweek*, May 1998) that the European Regional Development Fund has already awarded the scheme £4.5 million.

Perhaps the best theme parks actually have a theme which is more substantial. Recent history and technology are both ideal candidates, as are famous films. Film sets themselves may, in the future, be designated as sites which can be opened to the public. Space technology continues to fascinate: the Kennedy Space Centre in Florida, with its Apollo/Saturn V displays, is quite remarkable. Its centrepiece is a hangar containing one of the superstars of the space race – a gigantic 363-foot tall Saturn V rocket. Science parks, such as Futuroscope at Poitiers, are also likely to proliferate, and may perhaps turn out to be more enduring than other theme parks.

In a report published in March 1998, Mintel concluded that small family-run theme parks face an uncertain future, because of much greater competition and the need to make substantial capital investment in white-knuckle rides. The report also commented that theme park revenue in the United Kingdom had soared by 76 per cent between 1993 and 1997 to £231 million. Catering revenue doubled from £40 million to £80 million during the same period, with the average spend per head each year reaching just over £17.

The competition is indeed fierce, however, and the British Tourist Authority announced in May 1998 that Madame Tussaud's had regained the top position as the most popular tourist attraction, replacing Alton Towers (*Leisureweek*, May 1998).

Whether the 'dash for theme parks' will diminish only time will tell. If one views them as glorified fun-fairs then there is every reason to suggest that growth will continue; if one views them as means to communicate 'heritage' then there is every reason to hope that no more will appear. (Mercifully, the plans for a 'Merrie England' theme park at Corby did not materialize.)

Conclusions

Changes to the social context – to work, the family and to attitudes towards life itself – have all affected the leisure industry in one way or another. The appearance of a consumer-oriented society and a culture of possessive individualism have together created an expectation that leisure is a 'right' and not a 'privilege'. Curiously, however, the frenetic search for fun that one might expect of a secular society – being concerned with the here-and-now rather than the afterlife – sits alongside a Protestant ethic which is embodied in Western capitalism's espousal of 'hard work'.

Other world religions, notably Islam, have a different view of leisure, especially with regard to sports participation by females. Buddhist societies would be expected to adopt a less exploitative approach to leisure than societies which have adopted the type of Western capitalism referred to earlier.

But in a Western society, the demand for more leisure, for novelty, for instant gratification, for fitness-without-effort, could become a monster which grows ever greedier, and the prospects for celebrating the Millennium are evidence enough of what is to come.

However apocalyptic the vision, the leisure manager cannot change society. We have suggested instead that he or she can help to make it more tolerable, by being responsive. Being responsive on its own is not enough, of course, since the leisure manager must also be seen to be responsible, as the next chapter will explain.

References and recommended reading

The Economist (1995). *Technology and unemployment: A world without jobs?* February.

Finch, H. (1997). *Physical Activity 'At Our Age': Qualitative research among people over 50.* Social and Community Planning Research. (Also available from HEA.)

Glyptis, S.A. (1989). *Leisure and Unemployment.* Open University Press, Milton Keynes.

The Guardian (1993). *Not so young as we were.* 3 March.

Handy, C. (1984). *The Future of Work.* Basil Blackwell.

The Independent (1994). *Across the Atlantic: Grey power is the US secret weapon,* 9 July.

The Independent (1997). *The site that is bringing home entertainment to millions.* 26 September.

International Monetary Fund. (1996). *World Economic Outlook*. April.

Macpherson, C.B. (1962). *The Political Theory of Possessive Individualism*. Oxford University Press.

Merrin, M. (1998). *The Mickey Mouse outfit that makes a meal of our childhood. Daily Telegraph*, 4 June.

Mintel. (1998). *UK Theme Parks*.

The Observer (1997). *IT revolution in the classroom – but will 'National Grid' produce a generation of young cyber-potatoes?* 13 July.

Paffenbarger, R.S. and Lee, I.-M. (1996). *Physical Activity and Fitness for Health and Longevity*. The American Alliance for Health Physical Education Recreation and Dance, Research Quarterly for Exercise and Sport, Vol. 67.

The Sunday Times (1997). *U.S. builds jails for geriatrics to cope with surge in ageing lifers*, 13 July.

Young, A.Y., Skelton, D., Walker, A. and Hoinville, L. (1997). *Physical Activity in Later Life*. HEA.

2 The regulatory context

Questions

At the end of this chapter you should be able to undertake the following:

1 Indicate reasons why a leisure manager would need to have a reasonable knowledge of the regulatory context – and consider what 'reasonable' may mean in this instance.
2 Consider how sport in the United Kingdom and elsewhere is affected by the law.
3 Identify the Acts of Parliament, rules, gudelines, regulations, etc. which might apply to:
   (a) a large football stadium
   (b) a concert hall
   (c) a theme park
   (d) an outdoor activity centre offering programmes to under-18s.

Introduction

Finding an appropriate title for this chapter was not easy. There are a few excellent books on legal aspects of leisure management, written by qualified lawyers or solicitors, and of course they contain the word 'law' in their titles.

The approach of this chapter is both wider and narrower – 'wider' in the sense that it includes more than common law, case law and statute law; 'narrower' in the sense that, being one small chapter as opposed to a whole book, it cannot provide the degree of detail to be found in the aforementioned legal texts, some of which are included in the Recommended Reading list at the end of this chapter.

In any case, the depth of knowledge required of the student and practitioner will be different. Most managers in the past simply learned 'on the job'. They were promoted upwards because they were good at what they did. Suddenly, on being appointed as managers, they acquired legal duties and responsibilities for which they were often ill-prepared. Some discovered the full extent of their legal liability only when confronted with litigation in the civil (or even criminal) courts.

Nowadays, the situation is rather different, and indeed the courts expect managers to be aware of all the relevant legislation, particularly where health and safety issues are concerned.

Not only that, but courts will frequently make reference to 'standards which the reasonable person might reasonably expect to find', and thus there must be more to the job than merely knowing the acts, regulations and so forth.

Those who already manage leisure facilities are faced with slightly different problems from students of leisure management. Both parties must understand the general principles embodied in relevant pieces of legislation, and both should have a broad appreciation of the regulatory framework that is described in this chapter.

Managers then need to know the precise rules and regulations which apply to their specific establishment. The manager of a theme park or fairground, for example will be expected to know 'inside out', and to apply rigorously, the Code of Safe Practice issued by the Health and Safety Executive with respect to 'fairgrounds and amusement parks'. He or she should even know when the document is being revised.

The manager of certain outdoor activity programmes will likewise be expected to ensure that operational standards are in conformity with the relevant regulations (Adventure Activities Licensing Regulations 1996), as specified in the respective licence.

In both cases, the legislation is quite unequivocal, though the legal basis for each is slightly different. Technically, the code of practice does not of itself have the force of law, but any departure from recommendations contained therein can be taken into account if a case arrives at the civil or criminal courts. The licensing of outdoor activity centres is now mandatory, where they provide activities and programmes for under-18s, and failure to obtain a licence in such circumstances is itself a criminal offence, as defined by the Outdoor Activities (Young Persons' Safety) Act 1995.

Relevance of the regulatory environment

At this juncture, it is worth considering why some knowledge of the regulatory environment is so important.

We can identify seven reasons, as follows:

- an increased awareness of rules, regulations and potential for litigation, on the part of the general public
- an increased tendency to 'blame' (something, someone), which leads to legal action being taken against the 'deepest pocket' – normally the employer rather than the employee
- specialist legal advice being available to those injured in a 'leisure environment'
- sizeable awards for damages, made by the courts in certain celebrated cases
- the 'professionalization' of sport, which leads to higher salaries, and consequently greater claims for 'loss of earnings' in the event of an accident
- the growth in the regulatory environment itself, leading to the creation of standards which may be used to assess negligence in particular cases
- an extended application of the 'duty of care' notion, to include not only physical injury but psychological and financial harm.

Before looking at the regulatory environment in more detail, it might be instructive to look briefly at the seven phenomena listed above.

1 Increase in public awareness

Members of the public are generally more aware of the fact that there are rules and regulations which circumscribe the services which they use. Quite correctly, they expect to find a safe environment, where the risks are restricted to those which are anticipated.

2 A culture of blame

The notion that accidents occur as 'acts of God', or the gods, is no longer acceptable, where it can be argued that some person or organization was a major cause. If that person or organization is insured, so much the better, since damages – paid by the insurance company but ultimately by all who pay premiums – may well be substantial.

3 The availability of specialist advice

Advice may be obtained from legal firms which offer a service in 'accident claims', and indeed several specialize in sports-related litigation. Access to 'no-win no-fee' arrangements, as in the United States, is also likely to increase the number and size of claims.

4 Sizeable awards for damages

Damages awarded by the courts, consequent to a successful action, can be very substantial. Those awarded in the United States have set the trend (for the United Kingdom especially) by extending the idea of 'pain and suffering' to the psychological realm, and not just the corporal. Compensation payments for lost earnings, when added to those for psychological injury, can become vast.

Claims for post-accident compensation on this scale are sustained by the existence of insurance policies which cover employees from claims based on direct or vicarious liability. (The concept of 'vicarious liability' will be explained later.)

5 Professionalization of sport

Certain sports have always been predominantly professional, such as rugby league, whereas others have been predominantly amateur, such as hockey. Where professionalization is common, the 'loss of income' which affects the injured player is likely to be considerable.

The situation with regard to 'amateur participation' is somewhat different, though certain cases would seem to suggest that consequent loss of earnings (from normal employment) are also leading to very substantial damages. Similarly, the appearance of 'stars' in sport, created largely by television, has led to incomes which would have been quite unthinkable in the 1940s and 1950s.

To an extent, the same applies to the world of the arts and entertainment but there the careers tend to be longer, and the risks of physical injury fewer in number.

6 The growth of the regulatory environment

As rules, regulations, acts, guidelines, codes of practice, etc. come along, so there are 'yardsticks' which either a knowledgeable customer or opportunistic lawyer may use in the event of the service falling below that which was anticipated (or contracted for) or below that which is an 'acceptable standard at comparable establishments'. Such yardsticks can be used against defendants in cases where injury due to their alleged negligence is central to the action.

7 An extended application of the 'common duty of care'

At one time, the question 'Have I a duty of care to X?' was less problematical in relation to the leisure industry than it was in the workplace, since the latter involved a formal contractual relationship between employer and employee, and therefore the employer had an obvious duty of care.

With the growth of 'consumer protection' and the idea of 'product liability' – both to be examined later – came a fundamental shift in emphasis, which meant that an employer–employee contract was not the only such relationship which created a significant legal liability. Customers, participants, volunteers now all have rights which are defined by law, rights which are being vigorously pursued after an accident occurs. Sometimes, indeed, it seems as if injured people see their solicitors before they see a doctor!

The 'duty of care' principle now extends to realms previously undreamt of, e.g. to rugby referees and to personal trainers. Not surprisingly, sports organizations and governing bodies have expressed alarm at this development.

Application of the regulatory environment

The various acts of parliament, regulations, guidelines and codes which make up the regulatory environment for the purposes of this book are inevitably unique to the United Kingdom. European Union regulations are also mentioned where they are relevant to the argument, but not otherwise.

Not all countries have the same legal codes or underlying moral principles. The very notion of a 'common duty of care', for example, would become less meaningful as one moved further south within Europe. For the government to have a duty of care, there must obviously be a coherent nation state and a body of law which protects and compensates the individuals within that state. For individuals to be responsible for each other, situations need to be defined, laws enacted and remedies made available through the courts.

Health and safety legislation, as well as consumer safety legislation, stems from the 'duty of care' principle. The three 'regulatory acts' of parliament which apply specifically to the leisure industry in the United Kingdom – two relating to stadium management and one to outdoor activity centres – also embody the same principle.

Where the legal code is very different, for whatever reason, then this chapter becomes less pertinent. That said, if one looks at those inherent moral principles

– of which the regulatory environment is a tangible expression – then the material might still have a certain validity. 'Taking care of the customer' is a simple enough idea in itself, and must be acceptable whatever the legal context.

Whether the leisure environment has actually become safer in countries with such elaborated regulatory environments as the United Kingdom is open to debate, and one would need to examine accident statistics, levels of provision and frequency of use, in many countries of the world before reaching such a conclusion. My own view, on the basis of experience, is that there is indeed such a correlation.

Leisure environments in tourist-based economies (Cyprus, Greek islands, parts of Spain) or areas where tourism is extremely important to the local economy (parts of South Africa and India) exhibit particular difficulties, since those leisure facilities that do exist are not generally replicated for local people, and therefore have fewer regulations to control them.

If this chapter helps to remind managers of some underlying moral principles, as well as practical manifestations, then it will be useful in the type of tourist-based context referred to above. Neither neo-colonialism nor triumphalism is intended by recommending those principles which are evident within the legal code of the United Kingdom: they are for the most part easy to understand, even if their application may seem very complicated!

European Community law

EU legislation is gradually having a marked effect upon law in the United Kingdom, e.g. in the construction of domestic legislation, and in the granting of rights to its citizens (and other European citizens) which may thereafter be pursued within the United Kingdom's courts. On occasion, recourse is also made to EU law in cases where domestic legislation is ambiguous or unclear. EU law has applied to the United Kingdom since its accession to the Community on 1 January 1973 – European Communities Act 1972, and European Communities (Amendment) Act 1986.

Legislation made by the EU generally takes one of two forms:

- Regulations – which are 'directly applicable' throughout the Community
- Directives – which are, in effect, instructions to member states to devise acts or regulations in conformity with the Community's wishes.

United Kingdom law

Criminal law

The different courts for criminal and civil law within the United Kingdom are shown in Figure 2.1. Except for the Magistrates Courts, which also handle various non-criminal matters such as liquor licensing, and the Queen's Bench Division of the High Court, the two aspects of jurisdiction are quite distinct.

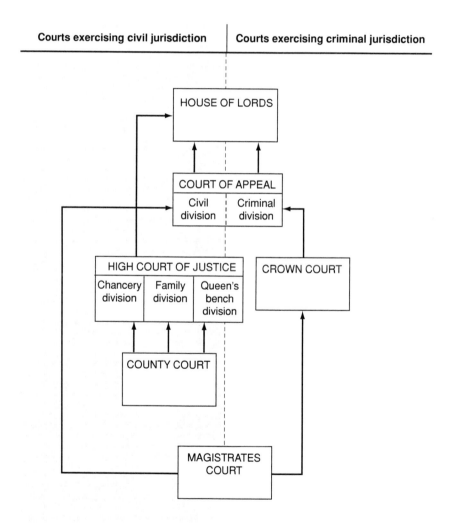

Figure 2.1   The courts of the United Kingdom

Criminal law is applicable where the state has previously determined that certain actions, or classes of action, are illegal. A 'crime' is therefore taken to be a 'wrong done against the state', punishable by a range of measures made available to the courts by parliament. The majority of cases are dealt with directly by the Magistrates Courts, with more serious cases referred to the Crown Courts.

Appeals against a sentence imposed by the Magistrates Courts are also heard in the Crown Court. Appeals against a sentence imposed by the Crown Court are for the most part heard in the Court of Appeal (Criminal Division).

Litigation within the criminal jurisdiction involves an individual or organization being prosecuted by the state, although in the United Kingdom there remains the archaic notion that the monarch actually 'is' the state, with no 'citizens' but only 'subjects'. Thus, the body that decides if a case can be sustained, and which actually takes the initiative, is called the Crown Prosecution Service (CPS).

Civil law

Civil law is applicable where one person or organization decides to take legal action against another person or organization. Commonly, such action is for the recovery of debt or for breaches of contract. County courts fulfil an important function in this respect, and may consider claims up to the value of £50 000. Where the value of the claim is £50 000 or more, the action is tried at the High Court. The county court's jurisdiction also applies to certain cases of bankruptcy and insolvency, consumer credit disputes, small claims, probate (where an estate is valued at £30 000 or less) and matrimonial proceedings.

From 'legal structures', we turn to look at some specific areas where the law has had such a profound influence.

Occupiers' liability: The 'common duty of care'

Definition

Legislation on occupiers' liability is designed to protect the public from harm, by creating a statutory legal duty from one previously embodied within case law and common law.

The concept was initially defined by the Occupiers' Liability Act 1957 (2 [2]) as follows:

The common duty of care is a duty to take such care as in all the circumstances of the care is reasonable, to see that the visitor will be reasonably safe in using premises for the purposes for which he is invited or permitted by the occupier to be there.

Relevant circumstances include 'the degree of care', or 'want of care' which would ordinarily be looked for by such a visitor, so that for example (2 [3]):

(a) 'an occupier must be prepared for children to be less careful than adults
(b) an occupier may expect that a person, in the exercise of his calling, 'will appreciate and guard against any special risks ordinarily incident to it, so far as the occupier leaves him free to do so'.

The duty was extended somewhat by the Occupiers' Liability Act 1984, to include trespassers – but only in certain circumstances, as follows (1 [3]):

An occupier of premises owes a duty to another (not being his visitor) in respect of any such risk ... if

(a)   he is aware of the danger or has reasonable grounds to believe that it exists
(b)   he knows or has reasonable grounds to believe that the other is in the vicinity of the danger concerned or that he may come into the vicinity of the danger (in either case, whether the other has lawful authority for being in that vicinity or not) and
(c)   the risk is one against which, in all the circumstances of the case, he may reasonably be expected to offer the other some protection.

The 1984 Act, significantly, stated as one of its aims; 'to amend the Unfair Contract Terms Act 1977, as it applies to England and Wales, in relation to persons obtaining access to premises for recreational or educational purposes'.

Relevance

All leisure managers need to be aware of this fundamental concept, i.e. the common duty of care, since claims for negligence are based on the proposition that the duty has been 'breached' by the manager, or by the manager's employer, or both.

The first question to ask is 'Have I, the manager, a duty of care?' In most cases, the answer is obviously 'yes', since a customer who enters a leisure complex may reasonably expect that complex to be safe. In other cases, the answer is not so obvious. Does the manager of an outdoor swimming pool have a duty of care to children who break into the pool compound on a hot summer's evening when the facility is closed? What if one of the youngsters is drowned? The position here is that a manager does theoretically have a duty of care, in the sense that he or she should have taken reasonable precautions to stop people (especially children) from entering into such potentially dangerous premises. Where the manager knew – or should have known (in the court's opinion) – that the fencing around the compound was badly damaged, then the court may decide that the manager was indeed 'negligent'. The 1957 Act does, after all, lay particular emphasis on the need for an occupier to be prepared for children to be 'less careful than adults'.

The second question is 'Has the duty of care been breached?' If an act or regulation has been ignored by management, then a criminal offence may have been committed. Notwithstanding, civil action may be pursued by the injured party, if it can be shown that the duty of care was not up to a standard which might reasonably have been expected.

The third question is 'Was the accident foreseeable?' Courts have a habit of using the 'reasonable' test in such questions. Would it be reasonable to assume that the manager of a theme park could have foreseen that an adult eating an ice-cream cone would choke on swallowing the complete object during the course of a 'white-knuckle' ride? The courts would probably decide that the manager could not have foreseen such an occurrence – but had the injured party been a young child, then the decision might have been a different one. 'Warning signs' (e.g. not to eat ice-cream during rides) are not wholly sufficient where children are involved.

The distinction is important, in that the law expects people over 18 to be largely responsible for their own actions, once the nature and extent of a particular risk has been explained to them. If an adult in such a circumstance does something stupid, then he or she may be said to have 'contributed' towards the accident, hence the concept of 'contributory negligence'.

The fourth question is 'Was the accident the primary cause of the injuries claimed by the injured party?' Judgements on this matter obviously require medical guidance, and by the time that the courts are addressing the question, it is out of the hands of the unfortunate leisure manager who is by now in the position of a defendant.

The final question is the one which ultimately determines the scale of the damages, and may be put thus 'what monetary value may be placed on the pain and suffering, as well as lost income, which arose directly from the accident?' Again, this question is one where medical and accountancy criteria apply.

At this point it is worth mentioning that the common duty of care does not impose upon an occupier any obligation to a visitor 'in respect of risks willingly accepted as his by the visitor' (1957 Act, 2 [5]). The question of whether or not a risk is 'willingly accepted' hinges upon a number of factors, particularly the age of the injured person. Generally speaking, under 18-year-olds cannot be said to have 'willingly accepted' risks in the same way as adults could. Increasingly, too there is an obligation for the manager to explain the risk in some detail, whatever the age of the customer (see also Chapter 7 concerning risks to customers).

The management defence arising from the idea of willingly accepted risk, referred to as volenti non fit injuria, is also mentioned in Chapter 7.

Disclaimers

As far as 'disclaimer notices' are concerned, the Unfair Contracts Terms Act 1977 makes it illegal to include special terms in contracts or in warning notices which have the effect of limiting liability for fatal or other accidents caused by negligence. No matter what the sign says, the manager and/or owner of the premises is indeed liable, if an accident results from a breach of the duty of care and is regarded by the courts as 'negligent'.

- **Relevant legislation**

> Occupiers' Liability Act 1957
> Occupiers' Liability Act 1984
> Unfair Contract Terms Act 1977

Health and safety

Health and safety legislation is really an extension of the 'duty of care' principle into the realm of the workplace. By so doing, it extends and specifies the responsibilities of employers towards employees, employees towards their colleagues, and of employees' own responsibilities for their actions or omissions.

Definition

The main piece of legislation is the Health and Safety at Work etc. Act 1974, which incorporated previous pieces of legislation, and which also gave the government a power to make 'regulations by order', as and when this became necessary. The power to make subsequent regulations has acquired greater significance since 1974, particularly where health and safety issues and food hygiene are concerned, simply because new technologies and work practices could not have been foreseen when the original piece of legislation was devised.

The purpose of the Health and Safety at Work etc. Act 1974 is described as follows:

An act to make further provision for securing health, safety and welfare of persons at work, for protecting others against risks to health and safety in connection with the activities of persons at work, for controlling the keeping and use and preventing the unlawful acquisition and use of dangerous substances and for controlling certain emissions into the atmosphere.

Duties of employers

Under the act, a general duty is laid upon employers to 'ensure the health, safety and welfare of all employees, so far as is reasonably practicable' (5.2 [1]). The employers' responsibilities include 'safety in relation to plant and system of work, the use and storage of substances, health education and training, safe working conditions and facilities for welfare at work for the employees' (5.2 [2]).

Under section 2.3 of the Act, employers must prepare and bring to the notice of employees a written statement of their general policy in relation to health and safety at work. Furthermore, employers must consult safety representatives of the employees and set up a safety committee, if requested to do so (5.2 [3]).

Duties of employees

Employees are expected to take reasonable care for the health and safety of themselves and others affected by their acts or omissions at work. They are also expected to cooperate with the employer, in connection with duties set out under the Act.

Regulations

Regulations made under the aegis of the 1974 Act are extremely important, and like the Act itself, have the force of law. Breaching either act or regulation may therefore be regarded as a criminal offence in certain circumstances (note the 'Lyme Bay judgement' referred to in Chapter 7).

Reporting of Injuries, Diseases and Dangerous Occurrences Regulations 1985 (RIDDOR)
Control of Substances Hazardous to Health Regulations 1988 (COSHH)
Electricity at Work Regulations 1989
Management of Health and Safety at Work Regulations 1992
Provision and Use of Work Equipment Regulations 1992
Personal Protective Equipment at Work Regulations 1992
Manual Handling Operations Regulations 1992
Health and Safety (Display Screen Equipment) Regulations 1992
Workplace (Health, Safety and Welfare) Regulations 1992

Other relevant Acts

Offices, Shops and Railway Premises Act 1963
Fire Precautions Act 1971
Fire Safety and Safety at Places of Sport Act 1987
Food Safety Act 1990 (see later section)

Relevance

Health and safety legislation – including acts, regulations, guidelines, codes of practice – has become increasingly important over the last few years. The need to 'protect the customer from physical harm' was always a concern on the part of management, but in addition there are now precise rules as to what 'standards' the customer might reasonably expect to find.

Standards recommended by national professional bodies, such as the Institute of Leisure and Amenity Management, or the Institute of Sport and Recreation Management, have also played their part. Ignoring their recommendations is not of itself a criminal offence, but may be used in court to show that negligence had occurred through the manager adopting a 'lesser standard' than might normally have been acceptable.

Similarly, although codes of practice may not have the force of law, either the 'defence' or 'prosecution' may use them in court where necessary. For example, alleged breaches of the 'Guide to Safety at Sports Grounds' issued by the Home Office, assisted the plaintiffs in their successful claim for negligence brought against Bradford City Football Club (Fletcher and Britton v. Bradford City Football Club [1987]).

The manager's role

Managers of leisure facilities are expected to make themselves familiar with the main terms of the Health and Safety at Work etc. Act 1974, with those of the other relevant acts mentioned above, and with those regulations which apply to their particular operation. They should also ensure that staff are fully briefed as to their health and safety responsibilities. Carefully constructed job descriptions are most important as a means to communicate the nature and extent of such responsibilities, and transfer some liability from the manager to the respective member of staff, according to what is 'reasonable', e.g. in the manager's absence. In other words, health and safety responsibilities should be made 'explicit', within a job description, and should not remain 'implicit' within a job itself.

Contracts

Contract law establishes and maintains a framework whereby agreements between parties or organizations may have legal force, and whereby breaches of such agreements may be remedied through the courts.

Definition

Contracts are now so common that they are almost taken for granted, e.g. contracts for a telephone, for a credit card, for hire purchase, for repairs to the car. Within this section, we shall be referring to contracts for goods and services, and not contracts of service, which fall under the ambit of employment law.

Examples of contracts

The leisure industry is involved in an enormous number of contracts, between clients (usually managers or their representatives) and contractors (firms which provide the goods or services).

At a cinema, for example, there may be:

- advertising agreement with a local newspaper
- printing of leaflets
- provision of water, gas, electricity
- hiring of films
- repair of plant and equipment
- occasional works, e.g. redecoration
- provision of telephone
- agreements with credit cards companies
- cleaning contracts (as distinct from the employment of cleaning staff)
- food/drink concession.

Swimming pools and water parks might have:

- printing and stationery
- food/drink concession
- foods/drinks vending (leasing) agreement, including maintenance
- provision of chemicals
- maintenance of specialist instrumentation or equipment, e.g. heat pumps
- hire of space, to local clubs and societies
- boiler inspection and certification
- cleaning contracts
- grounds maintenance
- purchase of fixtures and fittings, as necessary
- contracts (with members of the public) for swimming tuition
- contracts for sponsorship
- contracts for special events such as galas or birthday parties.

The lists are not meant to be exhaustive, but demonstrate the quantity and quality of the many contracts which might be found within a leisure venue. The more substantial and 'multi-functional' the establishment, the more numerous and complicated the contracts are likely to be.

What constitutes a contract?

All contracts are agreements of one sort or another, but not all agreements are contracts. So wherein lies the difference? For the most part, the law requires a valid contract to contain three vital ingredients, namely:

1   an 'offer'
2   an 'acceptance'
3   some 'consideration'.

In addition, the task must be 'lawful' (I cannot sue someone who fails to carry out an assassination for me) and there must be an 'intention', as well as 'capacity', to create a legal relationship.

The person who makes the offer (called the offeror) should understand what precisely is being offered, and be confident that he or she is capable of delivering the goods or services.

The person accepting the offer (the offeree) should understand the nature of the offer before accepting it. As the offer should be explicit (ideally but not necessarily in writing), so should the acceptance. An attempt by the offeree to negotiate different terms is technically a counter-offer, which means that the offeror can withdraw the original offer if he or she wishes.

'Consideration' refers to some form of 'benefit', usually financial, which passes between offeror and offeree. Money is not the only form of 'consideration'. For example, a sponsorship deal may involve goods being provided by a commercial company as prizes for a sporting competition.

Whatever the nature of the 'consideration', it must be 'tangible' in the sense that it has a value which is recognizable by the courts.

Breaches of contract

The leisure manager may end up at either side of a legal action for breach of contract, for whatever reason. Clearly, it is wise to avoid being placed in this position, if at all possible, given the time and costs which are associated with defending or pursuing such an action.

If action is unavoidable, the remedies may be summarized as follows:

- Refusal of further performance – where the 'injured party' assumes that a contract is either ended or rescinded by the other party to the contract, and therefore refuses to complete his/her part.

- Action for damages – where legal action is pursued by the 'injured party' on the basis of the 'consideration' had the contract been fulfilled.
- 'Quantum meruit' – literally, 'as much as has been earned', whereby the injured party pursues a claim (other than for damages) in respect of that which has already been performed, before the contract was breached.
- Specific performance – where a court order requires both parties to carry out their obligations.
- Injunction – where the courts agree to the injured party issuing an injunction requiring a part of the contract to be done, in instances where damages would not be appropriate.
- Recision – where the contract is cancelled or annulled, and where both parties to the contract may quickly be returned to their respective positions. Any misrepresentation – if such was a primary cause of the default – must have been unknown to the injured party at the time the contract was entered into.

Relevance

1 Contracts must be handled carefully, whether the leisure manager is the 'offeror' or 'offeree'.
2 Contracts should ideally be explicit (in writing) and not merely verbal, except perhaps in minor matters or for time/administrative reasons, e.g. for emergency repairs or telephone orders to a brewery.
3 Contracts should be based on the supposition that the client knows what is needed and is able to provide an adequate specification, that the contractor is competent, and that he or she is able to meet the client's requirements according to the specification.

Employment

Employment law provides a framework which defines the relationship between employers and employees.

Definition

It is important to understand the distinction between a 'contract of service' and a 'contract for services'. The former constitutes a contract of employment whereas the latter constitutes the use of contractors or third parties to fulfil a particular service. Thus the former is regulated by employment law, and the latter by contract law.

The distinction is significant for two reasons:

1   Legislation. Acts of Parliament, e.g. in relation to health and safety, or insurance cover, normally make the distinction between employees and the self-employed, where appropriate. For example, the argument of 'unfair dismissal' applies only to employees and not to self-employed individuals.

2   'Implied terms'. In contracts of service, there are duties and obligations laid on both employers and employees which are implicit, and which might not be explicit, for example, in a contract or job description. A contractual relationship between client and contractor whether for goods or services, is much less constrained, being largely (but not entirely) dependent on the nature of the contract between them.

'Vicarious liability'

Just as the distinction between the two types of contract is important, so the notion of 'vicarious liability' needs to be understood, especially in the context of leisure management.

Cases brought as a result of an accident may hinge on the notion that generally speaking, a person is considered to be acting in the course of his or her employment if the action giving rise to the claim was explicitly or implicitly authorized by the employer. An employee may still be regarded by the court as acting within the course of employment where he or she acts negligently, provided that the act, had it been done correctly, had been authorized by the employer. Only where there has been a clear and explicit prohibition on the employee doing something which is ultimately claimed to be the cause of the accident will the employer be free from a claim of 'vicarious liability' – in which case the liability falls upon the employee only. In practice, of course, most actions are pursued against employers, since it is they who, through their insurance company, have the 'deepest pocket'.

Relevance

Taken together with legislation on equal opportunities (see later section), employment legislation constitutes a substantial 'body of knowledge' which managers need to be aware of, in order not to transgress any particular term or condition.

Furthermore, employers who decide to take formal disciplinary action against an employee are strongly advised to follow guidelines issued by the Arbitration Conciliation and Advisory Service (ACAS), if only to avoid the aggrieved employee appealing against the outcome, or procedure, to an industrial tribunal.

Industrial tribunals

Industrial tribunals are one of several tribunals created by the Council on Tribunals, a body established by the Tribunals and Inquiries Act 1958. The tribunal consists of three members, namely a legally qualified chairperson and two 'lay' members. The latter are appointed after consultations with employees and employers organizations, though they do not actually represent those organizations and are not taken to be legal experts.

It is worth mentioning here that industrial tribunals are intended to be relatively inexpensive, informal and speedy in their application of employment law, on issues such as redundancy and unfair dismissal. Appeals against a decision of an industrial tribunal may be made to the Employment Appeal Tribunal, from thence to the Court of Appeal and finally to the House of Lords.

It is worth mentioning here that industrial tribunals may deal with the following health and safety matters:

- appeals against Prohibition and Improvement notices issued by a local authority.
- dismissal (actual and 'constructive') following a breach of health and safety law, regulation, or clause of contract.
- actions where an employer has refused to grant time off for health and safety training.

Relevant legislation

Legislation in this field is very extensive, but the following acts are important:

Contracts of Employment Act 1964

Industrial Training Act 1964

Redundancy Payments Act 1965

European Communities Act 1972

Employment of Children Act 1973

Social Security Act 1975

Employment Protection (Consolidation) Act 1978
Employment Acts (various: 1980, 1982, 1988, 1990)
Trade Union Act 1984
Wages Act 1986
Single European Act 1986
Trade Union and Labour Relations (consolidation) Act 1992
plus acts referred to in the next section on equal opportunities, where they contain clauses in relation to employment.

Equal opportunities

Legislation in the area of equal opportunities provides a framework to define and protect the rights of individuals who might otherwise be discriminated against either at work or elsewhere. Increasingly, the legislation is used in other (non-work) contexts, such as leisure.

Definition

The amount of legislation now labelled as 'equal opportunities' has increased greatly since 1970, and thus may be examined separately from employment legislation, although much of it is still predominantly employment related.

Early legislation related primarily to discrimination on grounds of sex, i.e. the Equal Pay Act 1970 and the Sex Discrimination Act 1975 (amended 1986). Legislation to outlaw discrimination on grounds of race or creed followed, with the Race Relations Act 1976.

Discrimination against the disabled became the 'third component' of equal opportunities legislation, at the implementation of the Disability Discrimination Act 1995. For each one, the definition of what constitutes 'discrimination' is included within the respective act.

Relevance

Sex discrimination

The Equal Pay Act 1970 was designed to ensure that a man and a woman employed by the same organization should receive the same pay and be subject to the same contractual terms, provided that:

1   their work is the same or very similar
2   their work is of equal (monetary) value and
3   in the event of a job evaluation scheme having been completed, their work
    was regarded as equivalent.

Other provisions within the Act effectively outlaw sex discrimination in collective
agreements, trade union rights, employers' organizations and professional bodies.

The Sex Discrimination Act 1975 (amended 1986) prohibited 'direct' and
'indirect' discrimination on grounds of sex. Covering discrimination in employment, education, provision of services, facilities and goods, the Act defines the
circumstances in which such discrimination is unlawful.

As private sports clubs are exempt from the Act (sections 29 and 34), it still
remains open for such clubs to be of 'single sex status' or to allocate a lower
membership status to either sex. This latter type of discrimination is the more
effective (or pernicious, depending on your standpoint) when the lower membership status is associated with the absence of voting rights – resulting in the perpet-
uation of the 'status quo' indefinitely. Some private golf clubs have been known
to use this ploy.

Cases involving single-sex sports clubs, changing facilities for female football
referees, and discrimination in other sporting spheres have hit the headlines in the
past, and will no doubt continue to do so unless the law is changed.

The Equal Opportunities Commission (EOC) monitors cases brought under both
Acts (1970 and 1975). Naturally, the majority relate to discrimination in employment, rather than leisure, but managers should seek advice from the EOC if they
are in any doubt as to the legality of any particular programme or form of provision.

Racial discrimination

The Race Relations Act 1976 made racial discrimination unlawful in the realms of
employment, education, housing and in the provision of goods and services.

While the Act has a noble intent, problems have arisen as to precisely what
constitutes a 'racial group'. The House of Lords decided that such a group may
have at least one of the following:

1   a common religion
2   a common language
3   a common literature
4   a common geographical origin

With regard to the provision of goods and services, the distinction between goods and services is still an important one. A section in the Sale of Goods Act 1979 provides, by means of contrast, the definition of a sale as follows:

> A contract to supply services, which may or may not include the supply of goods and materials, is therefore beyond the scope of the Act, since it implies that 'transferability' of ownership (title) is possible.

The Supply of Goods and Services Act 1982 extended some of the principles embodied in the 1979 Act, and also strengthened the hand of the consumer by placing obligations on those who provide services. For example, the Act provided that 'where the supplier is acting in the course of a business, there is an implied term that the supplier will carry out the service with reasonable care and skill' (13). Section 14 of the Act also provided that, except where a specific time limit has been written into the contract, there is 'an implied term that the supplier will carry out the service within a reasonable time' (14[sbp1]).

As in all such cases, what is actually 'reasonable' depends on the view of the court. It should also be noted that an EU Regulation, governing unfair terms and consumer contracts, came into force in July 1995.

Product liability

Liability for defective products has also been extended and codified in recent years. The Consumer Protection Act 1987 established the idea of 'strict liability', which means that the manufacturer of the defective product is directly liable unless he or she can show such a defence as is defined by the Act. The injured party therefore does not have to establish negligence.

Relevance

In general, leisure managers need to be aware that legislation exists in this important area, and must ensure that any goods which are sold to the public are not only 'fit for the purpose intended' as required by the Sale of Goods Act 1979 but are safe to use, in accordance with the provisions of the Consumer Protection Act 1987.

Legislation

Trade Descriptions Act 1968
Fair Trading Act 1973
Health and Safety at Work etc. Act 1974
Unfair Contract Terms Act 1977
Consumer Safety Act 1978
Sale of Goods Act 1979
Supply of Goods and Services Act 1982
Weights and Measures Act 1985
Consumer Protection Act 1987
Property Misrepresentations Act 1991
Sale of Goods (Amendment) Act 1994
Sale of Goods (Amendment) Act 1995
Sale and Supply of Goods Act 1994

In addition, there are approximately 35 relevant Statutory Instruments or Regulations, as well as a number of EU Directives.

Copyright

Copyright law exists to protect the originators of original works from unauthorized plagiarism or reproduction.

Leisure managers and students will be aware that copyright laws exist, though only the former will have had the salutary experience of being visited by a representative of the Performing Right Society (PRS).

Licences are in effect 'permissions' granted by the originator or by persons or organizations acting on their behalf, for the reproduction of an original work, e.g. a piece of music, a work of art, or a play. In some cases, the originator retains the rights to him- or herself; in others, that right has either been sold to a third party, or has been granted (under the terms of a contract) to an agency, such as the PRS which grants permissions and collects fees or dues, passing these in turn to the original originator or his or her estate.

The law of copyright is mostly contained in statute law, and in particular the Copyright Designs and Patents Act 1988, plus supplementary legislation.

More recently, the Council of Europe has initiated a scheme to harmonize legislation in this important area, particularly on the matter of computer programs, as part of the 'single market' operation. Outside Europe, the situation is more complex, and any transfer of ownership has to conform to the legal framework of the countries concerned. Where no legal constraints exist, then 'pirating' is almost inevitable, and has indeed become big business.

Copyright agencies

The various agencies which grant permissions, and collect fees, on behalf of the originators, include the following:

- Performing Right Society (PRS) – acts on behalf of composers and music publishers, in relation to public performance of their work.
- Phonographic Performance Ltd (PPL) – acts on behalf of the recording companies, who themselves recompense the artists with whom they have contracts.
- Video Performance Ltd (VPL) – licenses the public performance and broadcasting of 'music videos'.
- Copyright Licensing Agency – licenses the reproduction of specified visual material.
- Samuel French Ltd – licenses the performance of certain plays.

Relevance

Copyright law may be invoked where serious transgressions or 'pirating' of original works is involved. More likely, leisure managers will have contact with one or more of the above-mentioned agencies, depending upon the precise nature of their venue. In my experience, it is wise to seek advice at an early stage, rather than later, so as to avoid retrospective (and cumulative) payments.

Advice

The whole area of copyright law is extremely complex, but guidance may be obtained from the following:

- The Library Association

- The Association of Information Management
- The British Copyright Council
- The Educational Copyright Users' Forum
- The Music Publishers' Association
- The Intellectual Property and Copyright Department of HM Patents Office.

Licensing

While copyrights are special forms of licences, other licences are extremely important to the leisure industry. Those who grant licences, in these instances, are not individuals, but public bodies whose authority is derived from central government.

Public entertainment licences

Public Entertainment Licences (PELS) are granted by local authorities (District Councils where two-tier authorities remain, or 'unitary' authorities where not), under the terms of the Local Government (Miscellaneous Provisions) Act 1982.

Such licences are required for music, singing or dancing, where the event is 'open to the public'. Licences are also needed for some private functions. Whether or not the premises hold a liquor licence is irrelevant, since a PEL is granted in a completely different way. However, a PEL is not required at licensed premises which make entertainment available through TV or radio, or by not more than two live artists.

Liquor licences

Unlike PELs, liquor licences are regarded as matters of public order, and are therefore granted by licensing justices, not by local authorities. In effect, such justices are magistrates who are experienced in dealing with the various applications which are regularly received.

Many leisure managers are coincidentally 'licensees', though this additional responsibility is by no means automatic. The licensing committee often interrogates new applicants, and receives advice from the police as to the suitability of the candidate and of the premises in question. Local residents, if fearful of noise and late-night disturbances, may also object to a licence being granted – or renewed.

The type of licences which the justices may grant are:

- off-licence
- on-licence (public house)
- restaurant licence
- residential licence (e.g. for a private guest house)
- restaurant and residential licence (e.g. for a large hotel)
- club licence (for proprietary club, not a registered or 'members' club).

Justices may also grant Occasional Licences, to holders of on-licences who wish to sell liquor at a venue other than their own and Occasional Permissions, where charitable organizations may sell liquor at certain functions, up to four times a year.

Finally, with regard to this important topic, it should be noted that managers who are licensees carry a degree of responsibility which is 'personal to them' and not merely 'corporate'; their duties cannot therefore be transferred to another person, except with the consent of the justices.

Gaming licences

Gaming licences are granted by local authorities, for the most part under the terms of the Lotteries and Amusements Act 1976.

Smaller lotteries may be exempt from the procedure if, for example, they make up a part of what is termed 'exempt entertainment'. Private lotteries may also be exempt, provided that specific conditions are met by the organizers.

Where tickets are sold to the general public, the conditions are also very exacting, and the lottery must not be run for private gain.

Bingo is licensed separately, by the Gaming Act 1968.

Cinema licences

The control of 'film exhibitions' is a matter for local authorities, under the terms of the Cinemas Act 1985, which consolidated earlier pieces of legislation, dating back to the Cinematographic Act 1909. Some exceptions are possible, where 'occasional and exceptional' film shows are promoted no more than six times in a year, but the conditions of the licensing authority must still be met, especially with regard to fire precautions and public safety.

Any more frequent film displays will require a standard licence, but commercial cinemas in the vicinity may well object to one being granted.

Theatre licences

Theatre licences are a little more complicated, since unlike a film there are sometimes arguments about what exactly constitutes a 'play'. As with cinema licences however, a theatre licence is granted by the respective local authority within whose boundary the venue is located.

The Theatres Act 1968 defines a play as 'any dramatic event, whether improvised or not, given wholly or in part by live performers and where all or most of the performance involves playing a role'. For the purposes of the Act, a 'play' includes performances of modern dance and ballet.

Food hygiene legislation

Since virtually all leisure establishments sell food, either 'directly' by means of their own staff, or by means of 'catering concessions', something needs to be said about legislation which relates to food hygiene.

Public confidence in the food industry as a whole was considerably shaken by the BSE crisis of 1996/7, but a lesser known fact is that cases of food poisoning have risen dramatically in recent years, the majority related to Salmonella poisoning.

As a response to such an increase, and to scares over the safety of eggs and soft cheese, the government introduced the Food Safety Act 1990. The Act incorporates enabling powers, which allows any separate provision to be brought into line with EU Legislation. The Act also removed the notion that, in order for there to be an offence, there should be an 'intention' (to sell contaminated food), and makes it an offence to sell food which does not comply with safety requirements.

Conclusions

This chapter is probably rather daunting, more so for students – who feel they have to know everything – than to leisure managers, who realize that some rules are more important than others.

The way in which rules and regulations are increasingly influencing our lives makes a fascinating study. Initially, all of these were created in what was purely a United Kingdom context, but one now sees the increasing significance of EU legislation upon the leisure industry, as on all other industries.

Take one small example: in 1996, the European Court of Justice was advised that several regulations affecting the employment of football players in the United Kingdom were contrary to the laws of the European Union. Under a ruling, a player would be free to move to another club when his contract expires, without the new club having to pay a transfer fee. Such fees would still exist, but would only apply when the player moved while under contract. There could also be no limit to the number of non-United Kingdom players within a club, which again represented a change to the status quo.

It was argued by some football organizations that the ruling would completely destroy the country's transfer system, worth an estimated £80 million, and therefore seriously affect the smaller clubs, which rely on the transfer fees to raise money for improvements to their grounds.

Sport in particular is being influenced by legislation, it seems, not only from the EU but also from within the United Kingdom. Many stadia and outdoor activity centres, for example, now require a specific licence before they can operate at all. The idea of liability is constantly being extended, so that even referees and coaches need to protect themselves from litigation. (The former refers to the case of Ben Smoldon, who in 1995 successfully sued the referee for 'lack of duty of care' in allowing a high number of 'collapsed scrums' during a rugby match – one of which crippled Mr. Smoldon.)

Some leisure managers may well feel that this process has gone too far, that there are too many rules and regulations. At a time of 'information overload', they may consider that ignorance is a better alternative. The maxim ('where ignorance is bliss, it is folly to be wise') does not however recommend ignorance as such, but only implies that there may be circumstances where the condition is acceptable. Better far to have regard to the other maxim, that 'ignorance of the law is no excuse' ...

References and recommended reading

Collins, V. (1993). *Recreation and the Law*. E. & F.N. Spon.
Cotterell, L.E. (1993). *Performance: The business and law of entertainment*. Sweet and

Maxwell. (A text especially relevant to those specializing in the arts. See excellent chapter on Copyright, pp. 441–543, and on Licensing, pp. 579–625.)

Croner Publications. (1992). *A Practical Approach to the Administration of Leisure and Recreation Services.* (An invaluable source of information for leisure managers, though students would find it too detailed on certain aspects such as security.)

Grayson, E. (1996). *Sport and the Law.* Butterworth-Heinemann.

Scott, M. (1993). *Law and Leisure Services Management.* Longman.

Stranks, J. (1994). *Health and Safety Law.* Pitman Publishing.

3 Managing physical resources

Questions

At the end of this chapter you should be able to undertake the following:

1 Examine two leisure buildings which have the same or similar functions, but different designs and construction; thereafter consider how both design and construction affect maintenance.
2 Describe under what circumstances it would be necessary for a leisure manager to seek advice about the condition of his or her building and any systems therein, indicating from whom such advice may be available.
3 Indicate the range of knowledge and skills which a manager of public open space may be expected to possess.

Introduction

Leisure managers frequently have diverse responsibilities which include the management of physical resources. Such resources can be summarized as:

- land
- water
- buildings
- plant and systems
- equipment.

For the most part, leisure managers rise 'through the ranks' to gain their positions, and by so doing learn the hard way. Students, unlike practitioners, have the advantage that they may learn some basic principles of resource management well in advance, and may thereby avoid a few of the pitfalls.

Each of the five resources mentioned above has certain characteristics. The first two, land and water, may be described as 'natural' but much of the land used for leisure purposes has seen the influence of human beings, whether or not leisure is the sole or even dominant use.

Maritime leisure is a topic in its own right, as is recreation (or amenity) land management. In a text such as this, therefore, only the most straightforward aspects can be considered.

Buildings, plant, and equipment are all taken to be artefacts of human construction. The word 'plant' in this context refers to the mechanical, electrical and other systems which operate within the fabric of the building. 'Equipment' here refers to items which may be either 'fittings' or 'fixtures', depending on their usage and design.

It will no doubt be noted that 'air' is not included within the list, though it is a resource used frequently for leisure activities (gliding, parachuting, ballooning, bungee-jumping, etc.). Yet air is not 'managed' in the same sense, since it is not contained (as is a river or lake) nor is it generally accessible to the novice. In the United Kingdom, air usage is subject to safety regulations, to air traffic control and in some areas to military control.

Land

Land-based leisure activities include the following:

- rock climbing
- road running
- hill walking
- rambling
- abseiling
- orienteering
- pony-trekking
- mountain biking
- fell running
- snow-boarding
- skiing
- cycling (on road/track rather than mountain biking)
- car rallying
- caving and pot-holing
- sand-yachting

- gardens and allotments
- hunting, shooting and fishing (game or target).

Managing leisure land

Land may be made available for leisure purposes in the following ways:

- Access agreements onto private land, negotiated between private owners and a public body
- land purchased by specific bodies dedicated to improve public access, e.g. National Trust
- land purchased by specific bodies dedicated to nature (or species) conservation, e.g. Woodland Trust, Conservation Trusts, RSPB
- land given specific protection by means of legislation, e.g. Sites of Special Scientific Interest (SSSIs), and Areas of Outstanding Natural Beauty (AONBs)
- land set aside by private owners, as a result of government or EU policy, e.g. agricultural set-aside
- land gifted by private individuals to local authorities or charitable bodies, e.g. some playing fields
- land purchased by commercial organizations for leisure purposes, e.g. theme parks, holiday parks (once called 'holiday camps'), safari parks
- land owned by local authorities and designated as 'public open space' (subject to by-laws)
- Royal Parks (subject to some limitations)
- common land
- highways and other rights of way.

Land use

Green (1981) puts forward the idea that land use can be divided into three categories, namely the exploitative, recreational and protective. Each has its own objectives and characteristics. Even within a particular category, however, the potential for conflict quickly becomes apparent (see Figure 3.1).

Exploitative use

Exploitative use of the countryside takes place for either commercial reasons (cash crops or animal rearing) or as part of a subsistence lifestyle, as in smallholdings

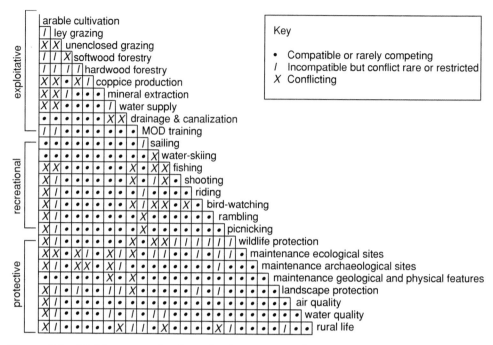

Figure 3.1   Multi-purpose land use in the countryside: a compatibility matrix of competing activities. *Source*: Green (1981)

or crofts. Included within this category would be commercial forestry, quarrying, mineral and coal extraction (open-cast), water extraction and storage. Military training would also be considered as exploitative, in this sense, although some areas are arguably given 'protection' – from farming and public pressure – by their military status.

Recreational use

Recreational use of the countryside could take place on either a commercial, public or voluntary basis. Commercial facilities might include fish-farms, shooting syndicates, and equestrian centres in addition to the more populist facilities such as caravan sites and holiday parks. Public facilities would include common land (where owned by local authorities), public open space, and other types of recreational land owned by public bodies, e.g. by County, District and Parish councils. Other facilities could be owned by voluntary bodies or trusts, e.g. the Woodland Trust.

Regrettably, the dogma of privatization, so rampant in the United Kingdom during the 1980s, led to Water Authorities – who own substantial amounts of land – becoming private sector companies. Their obligation is as much (if not more) to their shareholders as to the remainder of the population. Moves to take the Forestry Commission into the private sector were also a matter of some concern, particularly to the Ramblers Association. As it happens, the process (which began by stealth anyway) was not pursued to its ultimate end.

Protective use

Protective use of the countryside relates to objectives which are non-anthropocentric. After all, exploitative and the recreational usage can be seen together in the same light, since both take advantage of the land in some way, and both may have a disastrous effect upon the habitat itself. Areas maintained as reserves for specific plant or animal species would fall into the protective category, as would areas of particular biodiversity such as certain maritime locations, in the United Kingdom and elsewhere.

Areas requiring special protection will obviously increase as urbanization spreads yet further, and if damaging farming practices (e.g. use of fertilizers, deep ploughing, hedgerow removal) are allowed to continue.

A salutary example is the flower-rich hay meadow, now so rare in the United Kingdom but still to be seen in many parts of France. A newspaper article on an excellent National Lottery initiative to preserve 11 ancient fields at Oaksey, Wiltshire (*The Independent on Sunday*, 6 July 1997) pointed out that notwithstanding, the United Kingdom has lost 97 per cent of such meadows since 1945, and that they continue to diminish so rapidly that the remaining balance will be halved in 20 years time! The article quoted the director of the Wildlife Trust as saying that, by contrast, a new field was 'about as rich in wildlife as a car park'.

Conflicts of usage

Conflicts between the three types of usage are inevitable, due to the finite resource available. Conflicts, based on differences of opinion – and therefore of objectives – may also arise within any of the three categories. For example, recreational use of water will cause problems if one attempts to accommodate both fishing and water-skiing on the same stretch. Nor is a habitat 'diversity' as simple an objective as it seems, since associated maintenance inevitably costs money, and since some habitats (e.g. heather cover) result directly as a result of human intervention (heather cover is often helped by fires taking away the young trees which would otherwise shade out the plants). Even here, the 'desired landscape' is a matter of opinion, since there is virtually nothing left that is natural (i.e. unaffected by human animals) in the United Kingdom.

Countries such as France, Germany and to an extent Spain, are also realizing the significance of landscape degradation. Regional parks (Brittany), conservation areas (parts of the Rhine Valley), natural parks (Spain) are all features of countries where the Industrial Revolution perhaps had a lesser effect. That said, the United Kingdom still has a lot to learn: the extension of the M3 at Twyford Down, near Winchester, did irreparable damage not only to the chalk landscape, but to a government which had occasionally tried to look 'green'.

Tenure and access

Managing leisure land often involves the need to resolve issues relating to tenure and access, both of which are related.

Land tenure for our purposes can be seen as falling within the usual private/public/voluntary domains.

Ownership of land is not always easy to ascertain, though access to the Land Registry is now possible through legislation which makes the Registry's information more accessible.

The crucial distinction lies between land which is registered land and land which is unregistered, since under the terms of the legislation, there are significant differences between the two. Land owned by public bodies is somewhat easier to identify.

County Councils can own land, as can District/Borough Councils and Parish Councils. Equally, Councils can lease land to third parties, for certain purposes. Some local authorities own land leased to farmers, for example, and all have leasing agreements in respect of land used by local sports clubs. Since authorities are not free to simply 'give' the land away, they may grant leases of varying duration.

Voluntary bodies can also own land, provided that their 'charitable status', where appropriate, allows them to do so. With such ownership will come obligations vis-à-vis the membership of the voluntary body, and possibly to the general public.

As has been noted, all owners of land are expected to pay due regard to public safety, even where the visitors onto that land may be 'unlawful' and where rights of way cross the land, to ensure compliance with the relevant legislation (Rights of Way Act 1990).

Common land

It is estimated that there are one and a half million acres of common land in England and Wales. Ownership of common land varies: contrary to the popular belief, all commons are owned by someone. The National Trust, for example, owns more than 200 commons.

Commons represent an extremely important land resource, and are to be found virtually in every county: large areas of the Lake District are commons, as are the more 'controlled' commons to be found in Kent, Sussex, Surrey and Hampshire.

Ownership of commons by local authorities is extensive in these southern counties. Surrey has a larger proportion of common land in public ownership than any other county, and the variety of topography provides a welcome relief from the motorways and major roads which criss-cross the county.

All land is held subject to the law, and rights in relation to common land are especially complicated. Technically, the owner holds the land subject to certain Acts of Parliament and to the rights of any commoners which might exist. Thus the owner has main rights to minerals, tree planting and removal, sporting rights, grazing (where applicable), granting of easements (specific rights of access granted to third parties such as electricity boards) and initiating action for trespass. Commoners hold rights which are occasionally applied – defined by Halsbury (Law of England) as 'a right which one or more persons may have, to take or use some portion of that which another man's soil naturally produces'.

The status of a site considered to be common land may be verified by reference to the respective County Council (in shire areas), to Metropolitan Borough Councils, and to other unitary authorities, since it is they who by virtue of the Commons Registration Act 1965 are responsible for keeping the necessary records.

Rights of way

It should be noted that 'rights of way' do not of themselves create a freedom to roam at will or use the land in other ways: they represent instead a 'right of passage' from one point to another across the land.

Public rights of way are thus forms of 'highways', described by the Country-side Commission (1994) as follows:

- Highways which are footpaths may be used only for walking.
- Highways which are bridleways may be used for horse-riding (or leading), walking or cycling.
- By-ways open to all traffic are highways used mainly for recreation purposes but there is also a right to use 'wheeled vehicles'.

Rights of ways are normally held on 'definitive maps', and maintained by local authorities, in much the same way as for registered commons. Rights of Way Officers are employed to ensure that landowners keep to the rules embodied in the legislation.

'Permissive footpaths' are routes which walkers may use, with the permission of the owner. Since the path is 'non-statutory' (i.e. has no legal status) that permission may be withdrawn or modified. So as to protect the interest of the owner, there may be a notice advising users that he or she does not intend that the path should become dedicated as a right of way.

'Horserides' fall into the same category, i.e. they exist with the permission of the landowner, and have no statutory protection – unlike bridleways, which are statutory rights of way.

Access to open country

The National Parks and Access to the Countryside Act 1949 made reference to rights of access within 'open country', defined by the Act as 'predominantly mountain, moor, heath, down, cliff or foreshore' across which access agreements exist. Local authorities were obliged to prepare 'access maps' which amongst other things identified areas which could be considered 'open country' within their boundaries. The Act also enabled local authorities to compensate landowners where additional expense had been incurred to ensure access, and to use procedures for compulsory purchase where landowners were reluctant to sell.

Some open country is subject to a legal right of public access through local Acts of Parliament, whilst other parts, such as the Peak District, have secured such rights by means of specific access agreements.

At the time of writing, there remains the contentious issue of access, embodied by the slogan 'the right to roam', and it remains to be seen whether the government will be able to devise legislation which is broadly acceptable. On current form, and given the resistance of a powerful 'land lobby', it seems most unlikely.

Management by objectives

Strange as it may seem, all of our land is managed in one way or another, albeit with different objectives in mind. Farming is one such management regime – in reality a series of regimes, depending on the crops grown or animals reared – where the primary objective is financial survival, but where a secondary objective may be habitat maintenance.

Conservation objectives also demand that the land be managed, but of course the primary goal would be something other than finance. All SSSIs, for example, are required to have a management plan, with 'potentially damaging operations' restricted.

Recreational usage can require substantial degrees of management, according to the quality of the environment and the quantity of demand. Wear and tear caused by walkers creates considerable maintenance work in parts of the Lake District and Snowdonia, for example.

In order to manage the land, objectives need to be articulated, and planning undertaken. The quality of soil of an arable farm needs to be maintained, if the operation is to remain viable; the conservation area likewise requires a management plan, if its particular characteristics are to be preserved; the recreation ground must be managed and its turf carefully nurtured, if it is to remain a 'quality resource' for sport.

The influence of farming

The significance of farming to the outdoor leisure environment is evident enough: farmers maintain the landscape to a much greater degree than any local authority, national park, or government agency. Through their efforts, they have created much that we see today in western Europe, and take for granted. Upland farming in particular has kept the hill pastures and the moorlands in the United Kingdom from reverting to woodland – though in the more inhospitable uplands, such as the far north of Scotland, tree growth is restrained by wind, air temperatures and a reduced growing season.

Lowland farming tends to be a business which is seen as the culprit for the gradual degradation of the rural environment, aided and abetted by the EU's Common Agricultural Policy (CAP) which is regarded by many conservation bodies as both wasteful and ill-targeted.

In 1997, the European Commission announced plans to reform the CAP – which absorbs almost half of the EU budget, by channelling money to farmers directly, rather than supporting artificially high prices for their products. The Commission also expressed its intention to promote more 'ecologically friendly' methods of farming, and to provide 'structural funds' for hard-pressed rural communities – in some cases by encouraging alternative sources of employment.

The National Farmers Union (NFU) argued that such a move would cost United Kingdom cereal farmers £330 million in lost subsidies, beef producers £90 million, and dairy farmers £20 million, though these losses might to some extent be offset by the freedom to sell their products on a more open market.

Countryside degradation

In the meantime, and even as the farmers adapt to a redirection of subsidies, the countryside changes. The Institute of Terrestrial Ecology, using satellite scanning ('remote sensing') and selective ground surveys, reported in 1993 on the scale of the ecological destruction which had occurred in the United Kingdom between 1979 and 1990. They reported (*Guardian*, 20 November 1993) as follows:

- 109 000 miles of hedgerows lost
- 10 per cent of boundary walls destroyed
- 30 per cent decline in plant species on arable land
- 14 per cent decline in plant species on meadows and grassland.

Such losses cannot continue indefinitely, before the countryside does indeed resemble a vast car park, outside a restaurant at the end of the universe ...

Peace and tranquillity?

Consistent with the car park scenario is the discovery that another component of the rural myth is also unjustified, namely that of 'peace and tranquillity'.

The Council for the Protection of Rural England commissioned a study into precisely this aspect, with tranquil areas defined as 'places were sufficiently far from the visceral or noise intrusion of development or traffic as to be considered unspoilt by urban influences'. Thus, for example, a tranquil area would need to be more than 4 km from a large power station, over 3 km from the busiest roads, large towns and major industries, and more than 1 km from a main-line railway.

The results of the exercise were worrying, but received little publicity at the time. They showed that the South East and North East of England are those with 'least tranquillity', and that the South West is rapidly losing its tranquil character. East Anglia, once a relatively peaceful region, was also losing its tranquillity. The North West appeared as England's most tranquil region, and the least changed since the 1960s. Away from there, only North Devon, parts of Herefordshire and Shropshire, and the North Pennines represent significant tranquil areas where one may escape urban noise and intrusion (*Estates Gazette*, January 1996).

Blaming the farmers would be easy – but largely incorrect. Piecemeal and accelerating urbanization has caused the problem, more than any change to agricultural practice. Traffic noise, brought about by a questionable road-building policy, is not of the farmers' making, after all, nor was it they who severed so much of the United Kingdom's railway system during the 1950s and 1960s. A spectacular growth in air traffic since 1970 has brought about more noise, more pollution, and increased traffic congestion around major airports.

More cynical readers will recognize that 'peace and tranquillity' could result from a completely sterile countryside, in which an indiscriminate use of pesticides and herbicides has effectively banished many plants and animals from the scene. Such a prospect was eloquently described by Carson (1962) in her book *Silent Spring*. A similarly pessimistic view on countryside degradation in the United Kingdom was put forward by Shoard (1980).

Organizations

United Kingdom organizations concerned with land issues are as follows:

- The Countryside Commission
- The Forestry Commission
- English Nature (plus equivalents for Scotland, Wales, Northern Ireland)
- English Heritage (plus equivalents for Scotland, Wales, Northern Ireland)
- Rural Development Agencies
- The National Trust
- Council for the Protection of Rural England.

Also involved from time to time are the following:

- Association of County Councils
- Association of District Councils
- Association of National Parks
- British Canoe Union
- British Deer Society

- British Field Sport Society
- British Mountaineering Council
- British Trust for Conservation Volunteers
- British Trust for Ornithology
- Council for British Archaeology
- Council for National Parks
- Cyclists Touring Club
- English Tourist Board
- Environment Training Organization
- Farmers' Union of Wales
- Farming and Wildlife Advisory Group
- Game Conservancy Trust
- Greenpeace
- Inland Waterways Association
- Ministry of Defence
- Moorland Association
- National Farmers' Union
- National Federation of Ramblers
- Open Spaces Society
- Ordnance Survey
- Outward Bound Trust

Water

Watersports have a relatively chequered history but if one includes the sport of swimming in this category, then of course the management of swimming pools becomes a legitimate area of study.

The risks attached to the use of water whether the environment is natural or artificial, are obvious enough, but United Kingdom statistics show how relatively safe are swimming pools compared to the sea, lakes and rivers. Chapter 7 examines the relevant information in some detail, while Chapter 8 indicates some of the management responsibilities attached to the leisure-use of water.

Naturally occurring water

Maritime leisure contains a number of separate activities, notably:

- yachting
- dinghy-sailing
- wind-surfing
- water-skiing
- rafting
- canoeing
- fishing
- jet-skiing
- rowing
- power-boating
- plus the underwater activities of snorkelling and scuba-diving.

The United Kingdom network of canals is also used almost entirely for leisure purposes, i.e. for narrow boats. In this context, the role of the manager is complex: commercially, safety depends on matching a potentially dangerous and unpredictable environment to the competence of the customers. The water-resource itself is not managed in the conventional sense, because there is no 'containment' for which a manager is responsible, except in some instances for the condition of river banks and towpaths (see Chapter 8 on this subject).

In brief, the manager of a water-sports programme is expected to undertake the following roles (recognizing all the while that omissions in procedure or deficiencies in equipment may have fatal consequences, as with the tragedy of Lyme Bay described in Chapter 7):

- establishing normal and emergency procedures
- ensuring that staff are fully trained and have relevant (as well as up-to-date) qualifications in relation to their actual deployment
- ensuring that equipment is in correct working order
- ensuring that customers under 18 are given special protection from harm, and that over-18s are fully briefed as to the nature of the risk.

Artificial water environment

The management of swimming pools, diving pools, and other aquatic environments to which the public have a general or limited access has always been a matter of some concern, though as we have noted it is the 'natural' water environments which present the greatest risk.

Currently in the United Kingdom, all public swimming pools are required to have a measure of supervision, at a standard established jointly between the Sports Council and the Health and Safety Executive. The training of lifeguards is constantly under review by these organizations, and by the Royal Life Saving Society which administers most of the training.

Standards of pool supervision in other parts of Europe vary a great deal, but if there is an opportunity for review, managers might well look at what constitutes 'best practice' in the United Kingdom.

That said, neither in the United Kingdom nor the rest of Europe do 'non-public pools' seem to worry unduly about safety, and there have for example been some major accidents at hotel pools in Greece. Once again, the exposure to risk is very substantial, with a dangerous environment placed in proximity to relatively vulnerable people, mostly children.

And then there is fishing, one of the most popular leisure activities in the United Kingdom. Anglers use a variety of water resources, from reservoirs to rivers, and the activity has a competitive as well as 'individualistic' component. Angling clubs often negotiate fishing rights with private or public landowners, paying relatively modest sums for such rights but carrying out some management or supervisory roles in lieu of higher rent. Rarely is safety a major issue for this sport, except in instances where the risk is enhanced by the presence of particular factors, such as over-head power cables above river banks.

Organizations

United Kingdom organizations concerned with water management are as follows:

- British Waterways
- National Rivers Authority
- Water Authorities.

The main governing bodies of sport are:

- The Amateur Swimming Association
- The Royal Yachting Association
- The British Canoe Union
- The Anglers Association.

Buildings

Buildings are taken to be permanent or temporary structures created by human beings for a variety of purposes, whether domestic, public, industrial or recreational.

Buildings used primarily for arts, culture and entertainment include the following:

- theatres
- cinemas (single screen/multiplex)
- concert halls
- exhibition centres
- museums
- art galleries
- art centres
- civic halls (usually multi-functional)
- bingo halls
- dance halls
- night-clubs
- open air amphitheatres
- temporary structures (domes/shells/tents)
- film studios
- opera houses
- dance studios
- TV studios (audience present during recordings).

Buildings used primarily for sports (spectating and participation) include the following:

- ice rinks
- swimming pools (indoor/outdoor)
- water parks
- stadia (multi-function/single purpose)
- arenas
- ski slopes/ski centres
- tenpin bowling centres
- fitness centres/gymnasia
- squash racquet clubs
- boxing clubs

- leisure centres
- billiards/snooker halls
- synthetic pitches
- indoor tennis centres
- golf driving ranges/golf courses
- dog racing tracks
- racecourses
- indoor/outdoor athletics tracks
- go-kart tracks.

Buildings used for tourism-related purposes include the following:

- circuses
- fairgrounds
- theme parks
- zoos
- safari parks
- holiday parks/villages
- historic houses
- historic gardens
- aquaria
- amusement arcades
- laser centres
- marinas
- piers
- science parks.

Buildings where the leisure function is secondary to the main function include the following:

- school/college/university arts auditoria, sports facilities and galleries
- youth centres
- town halls
- church halls
- community centres
- public houses
- hotels.

The list is not meant to be exhaustive, but it does show how wide is the range of 'built physical resources' that one associates with the leisure industry. Except for facilities listed under the fourth category, where the leisure function is secondary, all of the buildings share the 'functional characteristic' that they are used for leisure purposes, and not for production, say, or education. The design and 'operational' differences between them, however, may be enormous.

A strategic approach to property management

Conventional property management has tended to regard 'built assets' as a cost burden, carrying an increasing maintenance liability as the property ages. Local authorities, in particular, viewed their properties in this way, since they had no 'asset value' against which borrowing could be made, nor could they be disposed of (except in special circumstances) on the open market. Such values do not appear in local authority financial reports – unlike company reports, where balance sheets show them as fixed assets (see Chapter 5).

Objectives for property management are important, whether the property itself is owned by the commercial, public or voluntary sectors. Clearly, any such objectives must conform to the strategy of the organization which manages or owns the property. Objectives can include the following:

- to provide a physical resource which is visually interesting, for public usage and enjoyment
- to provide a physical resource which meets current demands, and which can be adapted to meet future demands
- to provide a physical resource which maximizes the income potential of the organization whilst keeping the expenditure to a minimum
- to provide a physical environment which itself increases in value and thereby enhances the asset portfolio of the organization.

A clear strategy should be based upon identified objectives, and must ensure that the organization holds the optimum level of property in relation to its primary function, with neither under-utilization nor surplus in evidence.

Property appraisal

Managers are expected to know the quantitative and qualitative aspects of the physical environment for which they are responsible. They should for example, have access to drawings of the buildings, inventories of fittings and equipment, plus operational manuals which relate to specific items of plant or machinery.

A property appraisal should be thought of as a formal process, and may in a sense help to demonstrate the 'common duty of care' which the manager owes to the customer. Where the building is old, or of an eccentric design, or where faults are suspected, then the expert opinion of a surveyor, architect, structural engineer or drainage engineer is required.

Even relatively new buildings may be prone to problems. Many leisure buildings (particularly leisure centres) built in the 1960s and 1970s, incorporated clear-span flat roofs. They were simple enough to construct, and conformed to the factory-like demands of the time, where the facility was a 'product' to be produced 'off the shelf'.

Sadly, many of these buildings experienced early problems with water penetration, caused not by lack of maintenance but by poor design, defective materials or bad workmanship. The author once witnessed a national-class indoor bowls competition given added interest by buckets placed strategically on the rinks to catch rainwater leaking through the bowls hall roof!

Design-and-build

Some leisure buildings were also the result of a 'design-and-build' deal, whereby the client (usually a local authority) handed over the whole process of preparing a detailed specification, and supervising the construction, to a 'development company'. While this option seemed cheap at the time in terms of capital cost, the revenue implications only became evident much later, as more and more problems emerged. Because many of the original companies had by then disappeared or gone bankrupt, no claim against them was possible.

Functional suitability

The actual 'suitability' of the property is quite distinct from its physical condition. For example, a former stately home may be well maintained and therefore in excellent physical shape. When used as a museum, however, its layout may cause problems (of security, of visitor circulation), as may the loading capacity of its floor joists. These may seem minor matters, when considered against the appearance of the facade, but the architecture does little for the customer who follows a heavy wardrobe through the floor!

Functional suitability for sport is easier to assess, in one sense, due to the precise specifications made available by respective national governing bodies. Thus the

Lawn Tennis Association (LTA) will specify court sizes, lighting (for indoor courts), run-on distances and so forth. Where a specification of this nature exists, the task is merely to compare the building's spaces with what is specified. For competitive sport, there is no compromise: the pool is either 25 metres (no more, no less) or it is not suitable for swimming competitions (an Olympic pool is 50 metres).

The suitability of buildings for arts purposes is not so easy to consider, since much depends on 'ambience'. None the less, there are functional space require-ments, lighting needs, acoustic aspects and visibility which can be established within a specification. When the building already exists, however, mistakes are difficult to rectify. Any post-occupancy evaluation should incorporate the views of staff who have to operate the buildings, as well as customer opinions. The stage crew will often have a much better understanding of how their theatre operates, for example, than will the original design architect.

Trying to accommodate all artistic activities or all sporting activities within a simple complex is of course impossible. Where such attempts have been made, the result is usually a building which is perfect for nothing and most unsatisfactory for everything else.

Functional suitability therefore requires an assessment based on:

1 the relative importance of the activity being considered (i.e. 'ranking')
2 the specific requirements of those activities
3 the requirements of the licensing authorities as to building regulation, fire regulations, etc.
4 the structural integrity of the building, in relation to the purpose intended (in the case of a conversion).

Utilisation of space

The commercial sector is fully aware of the need to maximize the use of space, since by doing so it maximizes its return on capital, keeping its revenue expendi-ture 'per-employee' or 'per customer' to a minimum.

In reality, a 100 per cent occupancy is unachievable, and would in any case be most unpleasant. The levels of usage will be determined as much by health and safety requirements as by the intrinsic qualities of the particular leisure activity. In addition, space will be needed for circulation, storage, plant and equipment.

One common way of assessing space utilization is to use a financial yardstick. On this basis, the income-per-square metre will be a reflection of utilization, and this method is consistent with a cost-centre approach. A multi-purpose leisure facility would use precisely this method to assess the relative contribution of its component parts.

Compliance with legislation

Buildings must comply with the relevant aspects of legislation, as applicable generally or as devised specifically. In Chapter 2, we described some of the legislation which now applies within the United Kingdom, and which leisure managers in particular need to understand, given the unique nature of their job.

The following aspects need to be considered:

*   compliance with service licences (liquor, gaming, music, singing, dancing)
*   compliance with special venue licences (stadia, outdoor activity centres)
*   compliance with insurance requirements
*   compliance with internally established procedures (e.g. for emergency evacuation)
*   conformity with identified 'best practice'
*   conformity with regulations (e.g. Electricity at Work, COSHH, RIDDOR, food hygiene, fire regulations, etc.)
*   conformity with established standards (e.g. British Standards) and current Building Regulations.

All of the above can be considered in relation to the 'fitness' of the building. Does it therefore conform to the various requirements? Are any modifications needed to ensure current compliance? And would any alterations require specific approvals?

Improvement to building technology

Some significant improvements have taken place within the last half century. These may be summarized as follows.

1   Systems within buildings:
    *   energy-efficient boilers
    *   combined heat-and-power plants
    *   improved ventilation and air-conditioning systems
    *   development of heat pumps/heat exchangers

- computer-controlled instrumentation
- solar heating systems
- improved security/surveillance systems.

2   Materials and building technologies:
- development of improved polymers including PVC
- introduction of lightweight block work
- new materials for insulation (sound/warmth)
- 'system-built' component parts
- greater variety of specialist flooring surfaces
- roof-suspension systems (e.g. for stadia canopies) using bridge-building techniques.

3   Systems for safety:
- improved smoke/fire detection/alarm systems
- crowd scanning through CCTV cameras and monitor screens
- mobile radios and telephones for internal communication.

4   Technologies for entertainment within buildings:
- voice-activated computers
- computer-generated imagery for film-making
- computer-generated 'virtual reality' systems
- digital television and radio
- inter-active television
- satellite and cable television
- improved sound systems (e.g. Dolby)
- laser technology
- holograms
- compact discs.

5   Technologies for 'change-round' in auditorium form:
- hydraulic systems for staging/orchestra pits/seating
- retractable seating
- opening roof canopies (as at Sky Dome, Toronto).

From looking at aspects of design, we turn to the 'building fabric'. This section is largely descriptive but should help the student to understand more about 'building management'. Its three topic areas are as follows:

1   structure
2   materials
3   systems.

Structures

The most common structural forms are:

- Solid structure with walls constructed of brickwork or concrete, where structural stability is provided by the vertical form, including the transmission of roof weight downwards via load-bearing walls.
- Framed structure, with inter-connected framework of members, usually steel or concrete providing structural stability; an external envelope is provided either by cladding or non-structural brickwork.
- Surface structure, where strength is derived from a material which is shaped to obtain strength or stretched over supporting members.
- Air structure, where structural stability is provided by pressure differentials provided inside and outside the form.

In the first two instances there will be two parts to the building, namely the substructure and superstructure. The former is the structure below ground, up to and including the floor slab and damp-proof course. The function of the substructure is to carry the weight from the building above, transferring the weight to the load-bearing ground below.

The superstructure is all of the structure above, both externally and internally. Its function is to provide a suitable environment by way of enclosing and dividing space, whilst at the same time transferring weight safely onto the substructure.

The majority of sports buildings fall into the second category, i.e. their construction is that of framed structures with spaces provided by steel girders and external protection provided by cladding of one sort or another. Where brickwork is used externally, it may be either part-structural or decorative.

Some theatres built during the same period have adopted the same method of construction, whereas earlier arts buildings (and virtually all London theatres, for example) were constructed in solid form, as were swimming pools built in Victorian times. Museums and arts centres have sometimes utilized 'solid' buildings which were originally designed for other purposes, e.g. at South Hill Park, Bracknell, and Abington Park, Northampton.

New designs can also be problematical: managers of stadia or arenas are faced with buildings of an altogether larger size, often with design features (e.g. cantilevered elevations and hollow-section beams) which may be difficult to inspect.

Should managers be confronted with unexpected problems relating to the structure of their buildings, they are expected to seek professional advice. If the building is local authority owned, that advice is easily obtainable from within the organization; in the voluntary and private sectors, advice may be sought from an outside architect, building surveyor or structural engineer, on a fee-paying basis.

Materials

Besides knowing something of the structure for which they are responsible, managers should know about the building's component parts. These can be simply divided into metals and non-metals as follows:

- Metals: aluminium, cast iron, wrought iron, steel, copper, lead, zinc and alloys.
- Non-metals: ceramics (bricks, tiles), concrete, blockwork materials, timber, asbestos, polymers and plastics, bituminous materials, mineral fibre materials, plaster and plasterboard, fabrics, paint and preservatives, stone, vermiculite, cork.

Plant and systems

Plant represents the physical machinery (electrical and/or mechanical) which exists within a building, whereas systems refer to the 'distributed services' which follow. Any division between the two is fairly arbitrary, however, and thus they are here considered together. In total, they are for:

- drainage (foul/storm)
- water supply
- water filtration (at swimming pools and water parks)
- electricity supply (power points/lighting)
- emergency lighting
- heating (direct and indirect)
- ventilation (sometimes combined with heating plant)
- air conditioning
- heat extraction/re-circulation ('heat pumps')
- fire control systems
- smoke detection and alarms
- intruder alarms
- telephone/fax systems

- computer systems
- integrated systems.

Clearly, all of these systems are to be maintained in good order, if the building is to remain safe and secure. Where necessary, specialist contractors may be needed to confirm that the systems are, in fact, fully operational.

Maintaining leisure buildings

Leisure buildings are indeed extremely varied, as can be seen from the list provided earlier. And as leisure managers simply inherit their roles as 'building managers', implicit in the same role is that of 'maintenance expert'. We noted that both areas of expertise are merely assumed: they are almost always seen as secondary to the task of 'people management', whereas in reality the two areas of 'building responsibility' (building management and building maintenance) are extremely important.

Changes to standards in matters such as building regulations, fire prevention and glazing mean that certain forms of maintenance are concerned with something other than 'replacing like with like'.

The wear and tear experienced by leisure buildings may also be such that programmed maintenance is more expensive than for other buildings, having to be undertaken within specific closure periods.

Influence of design

Eccentric modern designs have played their part in creating problems within leisure buildings. Thus there are leisure centres where windows are too inaccessible to be cleaned or repaired, even though the glazing looks impressive within the architectural form. One sees – or rather does not see – voids between floors in swimming pools, wherein pipe work is totally entombed between concrete slabs. One sees post-war arts buildings, such as the Royal National Theatre in London, where the technology of poured concrete has created buildings which are virtually impossible to modify without vast expenditure on laser-cutting devices. The list is endless ...

Eccentricity of design also has an impact when a building constructed for one purpose is eventually used for another, especially where the former purpose was 'domestic', and the latter 'public'. Churches converted to theatres or arts centres, historic houses converted to museums, factories or warehouses converted to arts/exhibition venues – all show certain problems in respect of their maintenance, in that the standards of materials, of engineering, and construction will have been appropriate for the original function, but might not be adequate for the current one.

Legal considerations

Legal liabilities attached to operational management demand a very rigorous approach to the maintenance of leisure buildings. The need for vigilance applies equally to purpose-built facilities as to conversions, and requires that managers periodically check to ensure compliance with specified standards.

Building regulations consent, for example, is pertinent where alterations are being contemplated or extensions proposed. Improved standards of materials for fire resistance, of systems for fire detection, of emergency exits and so forth all need to be considered. Emergency lighting systems may need to be upgraded to meet present-day requirements, as may the glazing used in different parts of the complex. Again, materials once considered as suitable for building purposes, such as certain types of cement and concrete, and almost all types of asbestos, can no longer be considered as acceptable.

The concept of a 'common duty of care' (see previous chapter) makes it absolutely imperative that managers maintain their buildings properly, in conformity with 'best possible practice' and with those standards and regulations which have been established by law, or by relevant authoritative bodies.

Equipment

For the most part, the word 'equipment' is used for items which are provided for or by the customer, in order to undertake a particular leisure activity. Equipment can range, therefore, from a dinghy to a trampoline, from a saddle to a football, from a climbing-frame to a jet ski.

As explained in Chapter 2, a fundamental obligation is laid upon management to provide an environment which is safe. Defective equipment will inevitably prevent a risk over and above that which was anticipated by the customer. This is especially true of equipment associated with watersports, horse riding, trampolining and air-sports, where any defect may have catastrophic results.

The fundamental rules regarding equipment provided for leisure customers are as follows:

- only 'standardized' equipment should be purchased
- no modifications to standard equipment should be contemplated, except with the express (i.e. written) consent of the manufacturer
- only reputable manufacturers should be used
- whenever possible, managers are expected to ascertain (through the governing body of the sport, where applicable) whether a specific standard exists, e.g. for landing mats in the case of martial arts
- checks should be made to ascertain whether there is a British Standard or European Standard which is applicable, e.g. in the case of children's play equipment
- regular maintenance of equipment should be carried out in accordance with the manufacturers' instructions
- independent checks may also be appropriate in some instances, where risk is considered to be substantial.

Conclusions

Students need to be aware that resource management is an onerous task in itself, and one which is constantly under-estimated by people who work on a nine-to-five basis. Even some users forget that most leisure facilities are open to the public on seven days per week, for more than 12 hours per day. The resource-management should never be taken for granted, however, for reasons which should be evident in what has been said.

There is indeed a body of knowledge which the on-site manager is expected to know, and this is all too often learned once the person has been appointed and not before. In this respect at least, students have the distinct advantage of knowing what to expect when the time comes.

References and recommended reading

Brereton, C. (1991). *The Repair of Historic Buildings: Advice on principles and methods.* English Heritage.

Bromley, P. (1990). *Countryside Management*. E. & F.N. Spon. (See Chapter 3, legal framework.)

Carson, R. (1962). *Silent Spring*. London: Hamilton.

Cobham Research Consultants. (1992). *Countryside Sports: Their economic and conservation significance*.

Countryside Commission. (1994). *Managing Public Access: A guide for farmers and landowners*.

Curwell, S.R. and March, C.G. (1986). *Hazardous Building Materials: A guide to the selection of alternatives*. E. & F.N. Spon.

Glyptis, S. (1991). *Countryside Recreation*. Longman/ILAM.

Goodhead, T. and Johnson, D. (1996). *Coastal Recreation Management*. Chapman & Hall.

Green, B. (1981). *Countryside Conservation*. George Allen & Unwin.

The Guardian (1993). *Death by stealth in the shires*. 20 November.

Hall, F. (1995). *Essential Building Services and Equipment*. B.H. Newnes.

Harlow, P. (1984). *Managing Building Maintenance*. Institute of Building.

HM Government. (1995). *Rural England: A nation committed to a living countryside*. MAFF/Welsh Office/Department of the Environment.

Institute of Leisure and Amenity Management. (1996). *Health and Safety Guide for Leisure Activities*. Pitman Publishing in association with ILAM.

Richardson, B.A. (1991). *Defects and Deterioration in Buildings*. E. & F.N. Spon.

Shoard, M. (1980). *The Theft of the Countryside*. London: Temple Smith.

Sinnott, R. (1985). *Safety and Security in Building Design*. Collins.

Spedding, A. (1994). *Chartered Institute of Building: Handbook of facilities management*. Longman.

Stollard, P. and Abrahams, J. (1995). *Fire from First Principles: A design guide to fire safety*. E. & F.N. Spon.

4 Managing people

Questions

At the end of this chapter you should be able to undertake the following:

1 Consider when it would be important for a leisure manager to make a distinction between a member of staff's competence and his or her motivation, suggesting how either may be enhanced.
2 Indicate the main differences in the knowledge and skills required of a leisure manager, in the managing of staff, customers and contractors.
3 Indicate how conflict in the workplace may be utilized – or alternatively resolved – by the manager.

Introduction

The purpose of this chapter is to examine the management function, from both a theoretical and practical standpoint. We begin by looking at the management of staff, before moving to consider 'customer care' and finally at some aspects of contract management.

Managing leisure staff

Characteristics

Leisure staff have extremely varied backgrounds, and this variety – for groups at least – can be both a strength and a potential weakness.

Individuals working in arts administration tend to arrive at their jobs with arts degrees or HNDs. Those working in sports management tend to have qualifications in precisely that field, and many will have prowess in particular sports. Those working in recreational land management normally have a training in horticulture, but some have qualifications in woodland management or ecology.

Museum staff, as well as library staff, have their own specialist qualifications, gained at post-degree level. Commercial leisure organizations, such as cinemas, ten-pin bowling centres, night-clubs and theme parks attract staff from a variety of backgrounds, to the extent that it is virtually impossible to generalize about this particular sector, except to say that graduate/HND opportunities have been increasing in recent years.

In some cases, those with the same or similar backgrounds 'cluster' together, for example, in the world of museums and libraries. In other cases, such as theme parks and holiday villages, staff with completely different backgrounds will find themselves thrown together as part of the same management team. As one would expect, there are advantages and drawbacks to working in either of the two environments.

We begin by looking briefly at the nature of individuals, their own 'cognitive reality', their behaviour, motivation, competence, and also at appropriate management techniques. Before moving on to examine the 'job itself', we look briefly at the nature of group behaviour.

The individual

Individuals within the workplace represent human assets which if treated properly remain as assets but which, if treated badly, soon become liabilities.

Their personalities are made up of physical, mental, moral and social characteristics. Combined with their other characteristics, ideas, opinions, beliefs, attitudes and suchlike, they are sufficiently distinctive and enduring as to 'identify' the individual in question.

Two approaches are used to study personality: the idiographic and the nomothetic. The first assumes that an individual personality in its entity is what counts and is worthy of study. This methodology was adopted by Allport (1965), amongst others. The second, the nomothetic approach, looks at one or more aspects of personality, such as aggression, and endeavours to find both 'causes' for the behaviour as well as correlations with life experiences.

Managers must indeed have an understanding of how people 'function', how they behave and perhaps how they feel (about their comrades/the job/the boss/the organization). After all, behaviour patterns established in childhood – whether or not one accepts Freudian theory – are often seen in the workplace.

Individuals who demonstrate aggression or extreme cynicism towards the 'system', when in fact they can change the system, may be exhibiting signs of 'projection': their actual feelings may relate to a much deeper unhappiness. Similarly, some individuals when confronted with an important task will concentrate on trivial routine matters rather than 'getting on with the job' – or they may simply 'go to pieces' – a technique which may have worked when used by a child, but seen as 'regression' in later life.

Cognitive reality

Fascinating research has been carried out into 'self-perception' and the 'mental constructs' which people create. In part, the impetus for such research came from Gestalt psychology, which recognizes that the human mind seems to establish patterns, to perceive order within chaos, and perhaps by so doing creates a more reassuring universe. In seeking to understand the behaviour pattern of a member of staff, a manager must endeavour to 'get inside' the mind of that person, if the situation is so serious as to be 'job-threatening' for either party. Another person's perception or 'cognitive perspective' can be completely different from what the manager expects. A member of staff can feel undervalued and under threat, for example, and may exhibit signs of distress of one sort or another (e.g. absenteeism, heavy drinking, extreme cynicism). What matters in such instances is the 'reality' as perceived by that member of staff even where, in fact, it does not correspond to the reality of a situation.

'Internals' and 'externals'

Another useful idea in this respect comes from an early behaviourist, J.B. Rotter (1954), who surmised that all individuals fall somewhere along a continuum between 'internal' and 'external'. Internals, he argued, feel that they are 'in control', since they have 'internalized' their known world, and they can change things if they so wish. Externals feel that the world is beyond their control, that their thoughts and actions are of little or no significance.

Motivation

Motivation is often described as if it were a single entity, or a 'unified state', whereas in reality different people may have different motives for acting in what appears as a similar manner. If motives are 'inner states' that help to create behaviour, then they are often difficult to ascertain whereas behaviour may be observed. Martens (1987) put forward the 'double component' idea, that motivation requires both intensity and direction. Direction is represented by the choice of goal that will be aimed for and intensity the effort which is put into achieving that goal.

Motivation, for our purposes is perhaps easier to consider if taken in its visible manifestation, as an 'enthusiasm' (for the job) which is measurable through work performance, through responses (to new ideas or new responsibilities) and through body language.

Any psychological consideration of motivation requires a much closer look at internal drives, self-image (or the preservation thereof), goals and needs. Often unconsciously, we do assess motivational levels at work by the way that people (managers and staff) appear, behave, think and talk. We also tend to assume that a very enthusiastic manager or worker is competent at the job.

What actually motivates or 'drives' that person may to an extent be deduced from behaviour. Some people just 'like to please' (their bosses in this case), whereas others may be driven by a personal need to create a state of perfection which simply pleases them. The behaviour in either case may be welcomed or not, and it may be either appropriate or inappropriate to the work context. Being driven by the motive of 'wishing to please the boss' for example, may alienate the staff member from colleagues; being a perfectionist may alienate everyone if the behaviour is 'compulsive' (i.e. neurotic) rather than appropriate.

Competence

If motivation is assessed through a variety of criteria, competence represents an ability to get the job done. The word is used a great deal nowadays, either to describe an overall character ('he or she is a very competent receptionist') or to describe specific attributes ('he or she possesses a series of competences').

On either basis, competence is more fundamental than is motivation, in the sense that competence is a necessary component of the individual's behaviour at work, whereas motivation may vary day-to-day, or week to week, or whatever. Motivating a staff member will almost certainly be easier, and quicker, than creating competence where none existed previously.

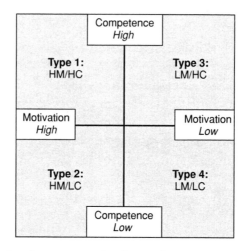

Figure 4.1　The interaction between motivation and competence

The relationship between motivation and competence

If we look at the relationship between motivation and competence, we may conclude that people will fall into one of four categories as follows:

1. High Motivation/High Competence (H/H)
2. High Motivation/Low Competence (H/L)
3. Low Motivation/High Competence (L/H)
4. Low Motivation/Low Competence (L/L)

The same grouping can be expressed in diagrammatic form, as in Figure 4.1

The distinction between motivation and competence is very important since certain management techniques or styles may be appropriate for one staff member but disastrous for another.

Management techniques

Experience suggests that the most difficult person to manage is not type 4 in Figure 4.1, as one might expect, but type 2. A type 4 individual may improve a little in competence if remotivated, but a type 2 individual will often be unaware of any shortcomings and cannot appreciate why any retraining might be necessary. Their very enthusiasm may also make them likeable, and therefore difficult to discipline.

Generally speaking, the management techniques appropriate to each of the four 'states' referred to above, are as follows:

1   H/H – The manager can afford to allow such individuals to get on with the job – the management approach may then be largely passive.

2   H/L. Because the individual is low in competence, the manager needs to ensure that key performance objectives are met – the correct approach is thus to be collaborative.

3   L/H. Motivation problems being easier to rectify than competence deficiencies, managers can remotivate staff by adopting a role which is supportive.

4   L/L. Where both motivation and competence are low, the manager would be foolish to adopt anything resembling a passive approach – indeed, the correct approach is to be directive.

The four management techniques identified above are useful, in that they remind one that there is no 'single correct style', but rather management techniques (or styles) which are appropriate for certain circumstances and/or for certain members of staff. Clearly, some circumstances demand a more directive approach, whatever the nature of the staff, e.g. on health and safety issues, emergency procedures and accident prevention, where the task is to impart the relevant information, rather than to discuss it, although some discussion as to implementation may be necessary.

The group

Most human beings work in groups, even if the precise form of contact differs. Individuals working at home may still, through E-mail, fax and telephone, engage in a variety of discourses.

The leisure industry is fairly labour intensive, and involves an enormous range of 'competences' or skills. Working in groups or teams is therefore the norm rather than the exception, and for the most part these groups involve physical proximity rather than telecommunications ('telos' being Greek for 'from afar').

Groups can be ad hoc – existing for a specific purpose, then disbanding – or permanent, formal or informal, primary or secondary. A primary group would be small in scale, with direct contact and close relationships between members; a secondary group would be more impersonal, with individuals perhaps representing the views of their base organization rather than their own.

Again, some ad hoc groups can be created to oppose a particular trend or action (countervailing groups) whereas other ad hoc groups may be established to consider options (the think tank), rather than a single solution.

Group characteristics

Groups have their own characteristics, of course, as do individuals. McKenna (1994) identifies these as follows:

- norms
- cohesiveness
- communication and interaction
- structural factors
- group dynamics.

The pressure exerted by norms is seen as highly significant, and we know that some members of a group will perform tasks – such as 'hurting' others – just because the group expects them to. Where the group norms conform to socially accepted norms, then this problem will not occur. Norms help to identify key values of the group, its functions, its traditions and expectations. Conformity to a norm can however cause difficulties when, for example, the group is behaving in a way which an individual dislikes, or when individuals pursue their own ends at the expense of the group – or indeed when the group as a whole is marginalized by the organization (the larger group).

Cohesiveness within the group might be more apparent than real. Many work teams, for example, exist simply because they have 'always existed', and the group meets because there is a 'meeting-slot'. In such circumstances, the apparent cohesion is an externally created phenomenon rather than an internally generated characteristic.

McKenna recognizes seven determining factors which interact to create group cohesion:

- similarity of attitudes and goals
- time spent together
- isolation
- threats
- size
- stringent entry requirements.

Cohesion should not be derived from purely external forces, but must represent the need for individuals within the group to express their own attitudes – including hostility perhaps – within a framework which still pursues the group's objectives, but which accommodates some acceptable dissent. Where people storm out of meetings, or sit glumly refusing to take any further part in discussions, then the other group members will feel some unease, because the 'acceptable norm' will have been breached.

'Spending time together' will normally help to create cohesion, if other factors come into play. Groups working under threat, perhaps of extinction, will also exhibit cohesion until the threat is removed or the group is abolished by the organization.

Where groups are essentially multidisciplinary or heterogeneous in nature, as in local authority leisure departments or theme parks for example, then cohesion is difficult to create. In such circumstances, 'management group' meetings tend to be fraught with problems of individual status – and any subgroup meeting may degenerate into little more than a 'therapy session' unless action is taken.

Social control

By exerting power downwards, and by establishing norms, formal groups exercise a degree of social control. However, the potential for control may create conditions where authority is oppressive. Fascinating but controversial experiments carried out by Milgram (1965) suggest that a sizeable number of individuals are willing to inflict pain on others simply because someone in authority tells them to do so. (In reality, the 'recipients' of the 'pain' were only pretending to be hurt by electric shocks.) Within such group situations, a certain number of dissidents would be required in order for the pain-inflicting role to be abandoned.

Under normal circumstances, groups soon develop a 'pecking order', in terms of the amount of speech and influence allowed. When the hierarchy has been established, meetings tend to become more predictable. Cooperation, rather than competition, should ideally result, but it appears that where one person within the group is to 'take all', then competition will remain dominant.

Conflict reduction

Groups also have a role to play in resolving conflict. Competition and conflict are different, in that the former conforms to certain rules and procedures, whereas the latter, being more 'general' in its nature, may eventually destroy the group.

Some conflict may be regarded as acceptable, if for example it engages two individuals within the group who might otherwise cause more damage. Again, some conflict is desirable, and seen as 'functional', whereas other forms of conflict may be 'dysfunctional' and ultimately destructive. McKenna categorizes conflict as: individual, group, institutionalized and emergent, with each having its own characteristics, sources and means to resolution.

'Managing conflict' can therefore be seen as a distinct skill, and Thomas (1976) indicated five ways to deal with the situation:

1   Competition – where the opponent is reduced in status or power.
2   Collaboration – where the opponent is 'taken on one side' and persuaded to collaborate on a particular project.
3   Withdrawal – where either side avoids conflict by avoiding situations (e.g. meetings) at which the conflict will be manifest.
4   Accommodation – where the manager 'gives in' to the other party, in order to keep the peace.
5   Compromise – where both parties sense that some 'give and take' is required.

'Group-think'

A notable characteristic of groups is the tendency for new ideas, valid criticisms and alternative suggestions to be 'smoothed out' in order to retain the consensus. This tendency is sometimes called 'group-think' and occurs in virtually all formal meetings as well as conventions.

Group-think exerts pressure upon individuals to suspend their own critical faculties so that group unanimity can be maintained. The leader's views tend to be less critical than might be expected, and the views of other participants are unconsciously affected by what they feel the group will accept or reject.

That said, the influence of highly articulate or high-status individuals within the group should not be discounted, and except where group survival is threatened, that individual may be allowed to deviate, according to an 'idiosyncrasy credit'. Views of less articulate or lower-status individuals, by the same token, may often be ignored by the group, even when their suggestions are perfectly reasonable.

Managers certainly need to be aware of the group-think tendency and take steps to offset it, however tempting it might be to preserve the status quo at all times. One way to change the 'power relationship' and to create feelings of ownership is to rotate the 'chairing function', for example, and to allow the out-going chairperson an opportunity to nominate the next one.

The organization

The organization in this context is taken to be the company, voluntary body or local authority whose portfolio includes the leisure resources referred to earlier, and whose management units are represented by formal groups.

Leisure organizations are primarily service based – they sell an 'experience'. Any 'products' sold are often secondary in financial terms, but both services and products may be of equal importance from the customer's perspective.

Organizational hierarchies

Human organizations which have a formal purpose and a degree of stability appear to create hierarchies at an early stage – one see this phenomenon, for example, with the creation of voluntary bodies, where the first task is invariably the selection of a steering committee.

Commercial (and military) organizations tend to create hierarchies so as to emphasize a chain of command, and by a process of centralization ensure that the organization is primarily task oriented. In the case of commercial companies, the objective may be to create maximum dividends for shareholders in the short term, or at least to secure a 'market niche' where this may become possible in the medium term, as with satellite television companies.

Companies which are production based would have a different hierarchical pattern from those which were service based. The latter would be expected to have more flexible hierarchies, with the forces of authority (the upper parts of the hierarchy) shifting from technical directors to accountants.

Pyramid-type hierarchies are useful for showing the 'span of control' which exists within the organization. The span describes the number of people directly reporting to the manager or supervisor. No ideal span of control exists, since the optimum size depends on a number of factors. For reasons of economy, as much as for psychological reasons, hierarchies have often become 'flattened' with fewer layers, so that the span of control is wider.

Organizational culture

The culture of an organization also tends to depend on whether it lies in the public, private or voluntary sectors, since the location crucially determines the organization's financial objectives.

Most organizations now have explicit objectives, set out in the form of their Mission Statement. Others have objectives which may be implicit or unstated, for whatever reason. Commercial organizations would be expected to display their explicit objectives in the body of their Annual Report to shareholders; public bodies might show something similar in their own Annual Reports to council tax payers; voluntary bodies might set out their objectives at an Annual General Meeting and in any promotional material.

While objectives, whether explicit or implicit, are to be taken as 'ends', the 'means' to achieve those ends are also very much part of the culture. Organizational cultures are fascinating, since the perception of the same organization, by individuals at different positions within the hierarchy, may be completely different. A manager may feel that the culture is open, democratic and fair to all, whereas an employee may perceive it as oppressive, undemocratic and unfair.

Formal messages which 'cascade down' the hierarchy are important, since they convey explicit information (e.g. on performance targets) which staff need to know. However the organization is also judged by staff according to the way it behaves, and not simply by what it says.

Organizational culture must be evident from a consistent behaviour pattern which is seen by all staff, and not just by the managers. A culture which is responsive, where messages travel upwards (to the top of the pyramid) as well as downwards, and where staff feel appreciated, is one which is most likely to achieve the best results, provided that other factors are in existence, in relation to organizational objectives.

Organizational objectives

Organizational objectives are vital if managers and staff are to work towards the same ends. Not only that, but objectives must be:

- clear and unambiguous
- reasonable and viable
- measurable by means of 'performance indicators'.

Commercial leisure organizations have an easier time with the third characteristic, since profit margins and dividends are a matter of fact, not of opinion. However, if one says – as many public venues did until the advent of CCT – that the centre (museum, art gallery, library or leisure centre) wishes to 'provide the best possible services for as many of the inhabitants of Utopia as possible', then how is one to assess whether or not the operation is actually a success? And what if each inhabitant of Utopia simply calls in to the centre for a minute or two each week – can this represent the greatest happiness for the greatest number?

Of course, objectives must be clear, attainable and measurable, otherwise they are not really worth having. Performance indicators must themselves be meaningful and relevant to the service which is being provided.

The job

It may seem strange that this section should follow that which has been said about individuals, groups and organizations, but in reality the job-held-by-the-individual is the nexus of all three sets of circumstances. Whether one is a manager, assistant manager, front-of-house manager, receptionist, publicity assistant or whatever, it is the job that matters to the individual, and the job that yields either rewards or disappointments.

Jobs in the leisure industry are extremely diverse, probably more than in any other industry. Given such a degree of diversity, what can therefore be said about 'the job' which is meaningful?

The following aspects need to be considered:

- job design
- job rotation, enlargement and enrichment
- job descriptions
- selection procedures
- performance appraisal
- rewards
- sanctions.

Job design

The job should be designed by people who know in some detail what is required by way of knowledge and skill. This may seem obvious, but all too often one sees confusion, simply because those who supposedly supervise the job simply do not appreciate its complexities.

The following questions should be put, in order that this job design is appropriate:

- Where does the job 'fit' within an organizational hierarchy?
- What are the unique characteristics of the job?
- What are the common characteristics of the job?
- Precisely what responsibilities are entailed by the job – for physical resources, people, money or information?

It may also be asked whether the whole job be done by someone else or if some of the functions could be 'hived off' to other staff?

Job rotation, enlargement and enrichment

Consistent with the notion of a 'standardized component part' is the idea that 'job content' – much diminished by the production line system – can be maintained through 'job rotation'.

Curiously enough, job rotation is quite common in certain sections of the leisure industry, and has a long pedigree in more populist enterprises such as fairs and circuses, where each individual undertakes a variety of tasks.

A second approach, that of job enlargement, is sometimes used for the same purpose, i.e. to create interest and maintain motivation. Job enlargement simply means that the work is 'horizontally expanded', to encompass work previously done by one's colleagues (alternatively viewed as 'they become unemployed/you work harder').

The third approach, sometimes called 'job enrichment', involves a 'vertical expansion' of the job, in the sense that an individual worker gains more authority, and therefore control, over inputs and outputs, so that the job is enriched through accountability and feedback, both creating a sense of achievement. (alternatively viewed as 'your boss becomes unemployed/you work harder').

Job descriptions

There are two conflicting views on job descriptions, one arguing that they should be rather vague, incorporating such phrases as 'and any other duties as may be required', so that (the argument goes) flexibility is created. The opposite standpoint is that job descriptions should be as detailed as possible, with every contingency covered by an exact phraseology.

The best solution is a compromise: adopt the second approach in respect of important obligations – the first approach, which is less prescriptive, can then be used for duties which, though important, carry less legal liability. This is especially true in today's litigious society, where leisure-related accidents are followed by substantial claims, as often as not.

Those who draft the job description, and make appointments based upon it, should always bear in mind that the document could become 'legal material' should an accident occur which results in litigation. Where negligence on the part of an employer or employee (or both) is alleged, the written responsibilities of a post, as set out in a job description, can become extremely important, notably to the plaintiff's counsel in a civil case or to the Crown Prosecution Service in a criminal case.

Selection procedures

Selection procedures should be conducted carefully and objectively. Those who make the choice should remember that they are also making an 'expenditure-decision' which may be as great as £100 000 plus, if the person appointed is paid £25 000 per annum and remains in post for four years before moving on. Before spending a capital sum of £100 000, one would expect to be confident that one has looked at all the options, and has drawn up an adequate specification.

While most employers still rely on the interview as a means of assessment, several larger companies and many local authorities now derive additional information from some form of testing. The tests, it is argued, give a more 'rounded picture' of a candidate, and provide what may be a more 'objective' summary than a 'subjective' assessment such as an interview. What can actually be tested? There are differing opinions on the value and validity of some tests, but in general it appears possible to examine the following:

- intelligence – using Intelligence Quotient (IQ) Tests
- verbal ability – through simple presentations or more complex reasoning/evaluation tests
- numerical ability – through arithmetical or logical-reasoning tests
- spatial ability – through visual-logical tests
- mechanical ability – through a constructional exercise
- manual dexterity – through hand/eye coordination tests.

Psychometric testing is sometimes utilized to assess 'personality traits', and some claim to indicate the likely 'management behaviours' which the candidate will adopt in certain circumstances (e.g. directive, supportive, collaborative, passive). If the candidate is to be part of a larger team, then such conclusions as to the role best played are obviously pertinent.

However, whilst it is difficult to fake intelligence or aptitude tests such as those listed above, either consciously or unconsciously, there is evidence to suggest that candidates undergoing psychometric tests are sometimes able to detect 'slants' in what the tester feels are neutral questions – and by their responses present themselves as more dynamic and purposeful than they really are.

Performance appraisal

Once a person is in situ, and the job has been done for a reasonable time, consideration needs to be given to performance appraisal.

Performance appraisal may be carried out by either informal or formal techniques. An informal system might be applied by a manager who at regular intervals holds a one-to-one meeting with his or her most senior staff, to see how they are 'getting along'. The meeting would be unrecorded, and there would be no direct connection with performance bonus or salary.

Informal appraisal procedures have the advantage of putting staff more at ease, but disadvantages include the following:

- lack of consistency from one interview to the next
- lack of consistency from one interviewee to another
- no obvious connection with rewards or sanctions
- danger of subjective appraisal, e.g. assessment of someone the manager likes may not give a true picture
- danger of the 'halo' effect.

This last effect is well known, and refers to the tendency of people (e.g. interviewers) to adopt simplistic binary positions, deciding in this case that someone (e.g. the candidate) is a 'good' person. Thus all the attributes of that individual may be seen in the same light. This is more likely to occur when an interviewer sees in the candidate a positive attribute or background similar to his or her own.

Similarly, but for different reasons, there may be a tendency associated with interviews which has the same effect: some people are very articulate and simply 'good at being interviewed'. This may convince the interviewer, albeit unconsciously, that the candidate is good at everything else!

Rewards

Pay may be the main reward which is associated with a job, but it is not the only one. In any case, there is some evidence that the motivational influence of reward, at certain points in a person's work history, may be exaggerated. A study carried out by Kohn (1993), in relation to incentive plans, concluded that financial rewards may have only short-term effects upon work performance, and will not alter fundamental attitudes towards the job and the employer. The problems associated with performance-related pay, and the various options open to a company wishing to introduce such a scheme, are well known. Experience has shown that no single scheme is perfect, and that some may even have a demotivating effect upon staff lower down the hierarchy.

Other financial rewards can be considered, as follows:

- Commission: usually a percentage of sales or net profit
- Piecework: payment according to a set rate/units produced/tasks completed
- Bonus: periodic payments based on overall company performance
- Profit share: payment according to a set percentage of the final profit
- Gain share: individual or group reward for cost-saving initiatives, e.g. from company suggestion schemes
- Company shares: individuals at whatever level may be allocated company shares as well as or instead of a profit share
- Share options: individuals (normally senior managers) are given an 'option' to purchase shares at current rates, in the expectation that their performance may bring about an increase to those share prices.

Non-financial rewards should also be considered. Some of these can represent savings-in-expenditure, and might therefore be viewed as income. They might include the following:

- free health checks
- free medical insurance
- free or subsidized membership of sports/leisure/health clubs
- subsidized canteens or luncheon vouchers
- company car schemes (loans or leased vehicles).

Sanctions

Human beings tend to react consistently to rewards, but the application of sanctions is a different matter, since some may cause a response which is quite out of scale with what is intended, and can go much 'deeper' than the manager who applied the sanctions may realize.

Recourse to a formal disciplinary process should be seen as a last resort, or as completely unavoidable, e.g. after a very serious breach of conduct. Managers are not expected to embark upon a Disciplinary Hearing until and unless the necessary conditions are met. Procedures followed should either conform to the organization's own, where these exist, or should follow the excellent guidelines set out by the Advisory Conciliation and Arbitration Service (ACAS).

Some managers use what are called 'verbal warnings', which may either be recorded on the employee's file or not, depending on normal protocol.

Alternative sanctions may be as follows:

- deferred increment (in the case of the public sector)
- loss of bonus and other financial ex-salary benefits

- reduced status to a lower post for a defined period
- deferment of promotion to a higher post.

Whatever sanctions are adopted by a manager, they should be applied fairly, in accordance with accepted procedures, and with great care. Rewards, whether financial or not, tend to work better than sanctions, where psychological 'reinforcement' (of positive behaviour patterns) may be required.

When the ultimate penalty is dismissal, managers are expected to be aware of the possibility that their judgement may be challenged at an Industrial Tribunal, and the employee reinstated. More embarrassing still, if a Disciplinary Hearing is used for an alleged criminal offence (theft, say), then the hearing's 'dismissal judgement' will look extremely foolish, to put it mildly, if the case comes to court and the individual found 'not guilty'. Civil action, by the employee, may well result. The manager is also put in a very difficult position vis-à-vis the other staff in the section or group.

Managing leisure customers

For the purposes of this particular section, it is worth mentioning very briefly what the characteristics of leisure customers might be, as follows:

- mixed-ability groups
- mixed-age groups.

In addition, there will generally be:

- high expectations of enjoyment
- diminished risk perception.

For 'open' leisure venues, such as museums, theme parks, pubs, commons, and historic houses, there is no way of predicting who might attend on any one particular day, and what their characteristics might be, by way of age, status and so forth.

Venues which operate primarily on a 'booking' system, or those where membership is a criteria for booking (or usage) can of course be more certain about the type of people who are likely to attend – even if they cannot always be certain of precise numbers, unless specific seats are sold in advance, as at a theatre, opera house or at some sporting events.

Choice and the leisure customer

Quite apart from the characteristics referred to above, the leisure customer arguably has more 'choice', in that he or she could, for example, choose not to go to the theatre or cinema, since neither is an absolute necessity. There is, in any case, a common acceptance of the notion that 'choice' is a right, and not a privilege (see Chapter 1).

Equally, some 'transferability' is evident with leisure, and the substitution takes on a different form, at a very different cost. If I am hungry, but poor, I may eat toast rather than trout. Either way, I shall have to go shopping somewhere, unless I am fortunate enough to own a trout farm or bakery – in which case I would probably not be poor anyway. 'Transferring out' is not an option with food shopping, as it is with leisure.

Leisure which requires effort and expenditure can quite easily be transmuted into passive leisure at almost nil cost. I may want to go to a concert at a major venue, for example, but if I cannot do so, then I may at least listen to the concert on the radio, or in some instances, see/hear the concert on television, or later on video. Leisure customers can often have recourse to the 'passive alternative' if they so wish, and if their particular demands can be partially met by means of radio, television, video, CDs, music cassettes, etc. Customers who desire exercise are normally less fickle, in that they wish to swim, or play football, or take part in an aerobics class or whatever. Rarely are these activities directly 'transferable', except in situations where no specialist 'supply' exists to meet a 'specific demand'.

The leisure market

The reality is that a perfect market does not exist, for a variety of reasons:

- Some sellers may collaborate to reduce supply and thereby increase prices (for CDs perhaps).
- Demand can fall for certain goods or services, without due warning.
- Demand will be affected by 'seasonality' for many leisure goods and services.
- Cycles of demand, over the longer term, appears to be fairly significant for some leisure goods, e.g. skateboards.
- Supply may be limited by external factors, crucially by 'what price people will pay', which is itself a function of 'disposable income'.

A 'subsidized market'

A subsidized market occurs when some external body, usually local or central government, interposes itself between seller and buyer. The effect of such a move is to reduce prices – which in theory increases demand – but by so doing the 'interposing body' helps to secure the financial future of the supply.

The arguments for and against subsidy are examined more closely in the Introduction, and the reader may find it useful to have another glimpse at Figure 0.2.

Subsidized markets do obviously assist customers in the short term, simply by reducing prices, and some 'complete subsidies' (i.e. 100 per cent) are applied for purely practical reasons. It makes no sense to pay someone a salary to take money from members of the public who merely wish to take a walk in the park, for example.

Some leisure customers therefore benefit from subsidies, whereas some do not. A cinema ticket is not subsidized, except in the very few regional film theatres, whereas a ticket to the opera is likely to be, either through subsidy to the venue or to the opera company.

The voluntary leisure sector is a different matter, in that individuals do not make a charge for services which would otherwise appear as expenditure items on the annual accounts. Such generosity is not generally viewed as 'subsidy', although like subsidy it has the effect of lowering prices to participants.

The customer as a financial resource

Income, for the most part, depends on a series of individuals deciding to participate in a specific leisure pursuit or visit a specific leisure venue. Any number of inhibitory factors may intervene to change their minds, such as:

- diminished disposable income, e.g. through unemployment
- the prospect of diminished disposable income, e.g. through job insecurity
- the availability of cheaper alternatives
- 'transferability of choice' to another 'product', e.g. from a leisure centre to a fitness club
- inclement weather conditions
- diminished time availability, e.g. through pressure of work.

The point here is that a leisure facility's income is an aggregate of many hundreds or thousands of 'individual commitments', which might easily have been deflected elsewhere.

And of course if no such commitments are made, then both primary and secondary income are affected. In the public sector, subsidy may come into play, in order to inject additional income into the equation, but the private sector cannot rely on such generosity, having to consider short-term borrowing, perhaps renegotiating terms for existing loans, to ensure financial survival.

Whereas income is hypothetical until individuals pay their money, expenditure is not so, since there will be contractual commitments which demand regular expenditure payments, e.g. for staff wages/salaries, for electricity, water, insurance and so on. As we shall see in Chapter 5, an organization's cash flow is just as important as its annual budget – possibly more so in the leisure business, where borrowing can be very difficult and expensive, and where seasonality can be so significant a factor.

Customer care is therefore of fundamental importance in the leisure industry, since there are so many inhibiting factors to the 'leisure spend', and since in any case that spend could quite easily be committed elsewhere.

Principles of customer care

The notion of customer care is not new, but the two words are nowadays used in tandem to create a concept which is of crucial significance.

Central to the concept is the belief that the customer is paramount ('the customer is king'), and that the customer is to be treated as such by the seller of goods or services. Of course, this concept is tempered by an appreciation that customers do not always know what they want, or how to make choices between A and B – but on the whole the concept is accepted in societies which have capitalist economies and a tradition of 'possessive individualism'.

Aspects of customer care

Customers expect the following set of circumstances to be present during their visit:

- value for money, in terms of quantity and quality
- the experience as described
- protection from physical harm
- security of goods and belongings
- quality of ancillary services and goods
- positive signals.

Value for money

What constitutes value for money is only definable in terms of personal experience, and a difficulty is that preferences ('demands') in leisure are more divergent than in many other industries. 'Value', in this context, is not absolute, but relates to the benefits received, in proportion to the total of disposable income.

Secondary as well as primary spend is taken into account by visitors to facilities such as water parks, theme parks and safari parks. 'Good value for money' may be a phrase which relates to 'total expenditure' (even if this is quite substantial), as being preferable to the less predictable expenditure at ordinary fun-fairs and zoos. Certainly, theme parks such as those referred to in Chapter 1 benefit from the 'all-inclusive' principle, where rides and other adventures are paid for within the admission charge.

'Value for money' must, in the end, be a matter for customers to determine, and it may be assumed that 'repeat visits' are one means by which that judgement can be measured.

The experience as described

Customers expect to get what they pay for, and are annoyed when conditions are otherwise than those anticipated. Where the experience is akin to a 'product', then this is quite understandable. After all, if I buy a ticket to see Edward II and turn up at the theatre, only to be told that it is Hobson's Choice (in all senses), then I should be less than satisfied.

If, however, I attend a circus, or visit a restaurant, or a theme park or a race-meeting – what am I really to expect? Where I am merely an observer, and not a participant, I can expect a reasonable standard of performance or presentation. This must be as true for rock concerts as for rugby matches. After all, consumer protection legislation and contract law protect me from buying something which has been 'misrepresented'.

Where I am a participant in the overall experience, or at least where my physical participation is an essential part of the experience, then the issue is more complicated. My perceptions will be more a matter of subjective opinion, rather than of objective fact. A white-knuckle ride may be perceived as extremely exciting by one person, and rather tame by another.

From a legal standpoint, I expect to receive that which is advertised, on the basis of which I have paid my entrance money and thereby entered into a contract with the 'provider' (or seller) of the leisure experience.

Where risk is an intrinsic part of the deal, then I also expect to experience the excitement of that risk – only that risk, and not the risk of 'uncontrolled descents' (caused by the parachute failing to open) or 'mechanical failure' (followed by an awful drop). In other words, I have very specific expectations of what I have purchased, even where they may be an element of risk.

Protection from physical harm

Consistent with the idea of 'getting what you pay for', or 'the experience as described' is the notion that the risks – where these constitute part of the leisure experience – should ideally be no less, and certainly no more, than those which were anticipated by the customer.

This particular notion has always been an implicit part of 'fairground experiences', of 'roller coasters', 'twisters' and now 'white-knuckle rides' of different types. As we shall see, the human behaviour aspect, which itself may accentuate risk, is in such circumstances increasingly restricted through physical means. Thus, for example, passengers on high-speed rides are held in place by a restraining rigid harness which prevents the body from significant movement.

Chapter 2 explains in some detail the legal concept known as the 'common duty of care', and the section dealing with the concept might usefully be read in conjunction with this section.

One defence against a charge of negligence is that the customer knew or 'volunteered' to take the risk, and is called upon in cases where adults are injured whilst playing sport. The Latin tag volenti non fit injuria, has often been claimed in such instances (the phrase means 'volunteering does not make for injury') but in recent years the law has moved towards greater consumer protection, especially in the United Kingdom.

To argue that someone 'accepted the risk' presupposes that they understand the risk in some detail – which is why the 'volenti' defence is less effective in cases where a person under 18 is injured in an accident, as a result of the management's negligence.

Warning notices have become more common, as have notices which endeavour to restrict the scope of the management's liability (see the reference, however, to Unfair Contract Terms Act 1977, in Chapter 2). Undoubtedly, such notices help to support the management defence that the customer was warned, but how far should this process proceed? If the medical world is anything to go by, then perhaps a 'probability notice' might be required, saying 'You have 10 000 : 1 chance of being seriously injured on this ride, and a 100 000 : 1 chance of being killed'.

The point is exaggerated, perhaps, but is not entirely spurious since the precise wording of warning notices has grown more significant of late, constituting part of some legal defences.

Security of goods and belongings

Customers expect that their goods and belongings will be protected, during the time that they remain within the facility. Whilst the management may consider the car parking area to be a lesser responsibility in this regard, customers none the less anticipate that their vehicles will have some protection, and that the goods within their vehicles will be there when they return.

Whilst 'disclaimer' signs for accidents caused through management negligence are meaningless, in legal terms, signs that advise customers not to leave valuables in their vehicles, or in lockers, do have their purpose, and the management is thereby in a stronger position should the vehicle, or locker, be broken into and something valuable taken.

Quality of ancillary services and goods

As all managers should be aware, it is the 'customer perception' which counts, and not the 'objective reality'. That being so, the totality of the leisure experience is important, and not just one part. Often, indeed, it is the ancillary facilities which become more significant in situations where competition increases: thus, for example, an airline company will provide in-flight hospitality which is better than that of its rivals, in the knowledge that this 'makes the difference' to the customer.

Expectations, motivation, perceptions and assessment are all determinants of customer behaviour, and cannot entirely be predicted. To make matters more complicated, different customers will have different expectations, motivations, perceptions and assessments from each other, as might even the same customer at a different stage of his or her life.

'Quality' in respect of ancillary services and goods also encompasses value-for-money, and those venues which offer on-site bars, cafés or restaurants should resist the temptation to extract as much secondary income as possible. The customer may well 'pay up' because the kids are hungry – but the family will never return.

Similarly, incidental goods sold at leisure venues should represent good value-for-money, should be of 'merchantable' quality (Sale of Goods Act 1979) or of a quality which might reasonably be expected (Sale and Supply of Goods Act 1994) and should be chosen carefully by the management so that their quality is consistent. The

National Trust, for example, exercises a degree of quality control which ensures such consistency – though its retail outlets all look much the same, as a result.

Services on-site must also be well organized, with personnel trained in relevant aspects of customer care. Equally, such training cannot be effective unless the staff themselves feel 'cared for' by management.

Positive signals

Positive signals refer to those characteristics which make the experience 'worth-while', and which encourage the customer to make a repeat visit.

Accepting that customers may have different perceptions, and therefore assessment, of the same facility, there are nonetheless positive stimuli which together influence the final outcome. Supermarkets are well aware of the need to create a 'positive signal' at the outset of the shopping experience – which is why fruit and vegetables are placed near the store entrance, where customers may handle (to an extent) and choose products.

Rice (1993) refers to market research which shows that 'sensory thresholds' are very important in such instances. These can be categorized as follows:

1   An absolute threshold – the minimum level at which the sensation is experienced.
2   A differential threshold – the point at which the gap between stimuli is sufficiently great for disparity to be noticeable.
3   Dual thresholds – where some senses seem to have quite different thresholds.

Positive signals from an experience must, of course, outweigh negative ones, if the customer is to make a return visit.

Handling customer complaints

Customer complaint procedures, and the very act of obtaining customer opinions, also help to send out positive signals. Where complaints are properly received, and correctly dealt with – and possibly some recompense made for a bad experience – then evidence suggests that the customer will return.

It is generally accepted by the tourism industry that the following responses occur:

*   90 per cent of dissatisfied customers never complain – but they tell nine other people how poor the service was.

- 13 per cent of those will tell at least 20 others.
- 90 per cent of the originally dissatisfied customers will never return.

The message, therefore, is obvious enough: managers should not only ensure that customers are satisfied, but also, if they do complain, deal with those complaints properly. A procedure for handling complaints may be summarized as follows:

- Allow the customer to have his or her say.
- Demonstrate that the complaint is taken seriously, where appropriate, e.g. by body language, attentiveness, discussing the matter at some length.
- Investigate the complaint – if the complaint is against a member of staff, managers are not to assume that the customer's word alone represents sufficient grounds for disciplinary action (see previous reference to disciplinary procedures).
- Advise the customer of the conclusion, and any corrective action which has been taken. If the complaint involves physical harm of some sort, care should be taken not to admit liability, even if the manager privately believes that the organization was largely to blame.
- Compensate the customer, wherever possible, e.g. free tickets to the next show, free swimming for one week, or whatever. The compensation should be commensurate with the complaint, for if misjudged will make matters worse.

Complaints against members of staff are especially difficult to handle: if the manager sides entirely with the customer ('I never trusted X anyway') then this will complicate matters if it turns out that the customer is, in fact, at fault. Equally, criticising one's own staff for lack of competence creates a very poor impression of the way the organization is managed.

Serious complaints, of theft or assault, will necessitate police involvement, but here again the managers are expected to ascertain the facts and not jump to conclusions. Customers need to be advised that independent witnesses would almost certainly be needed, should the case come to court. Managers also need to bear in mind that once called in to investigate a case, the police cannot be 'disengaged' by the management.

Customer preconceptions

Preconceived ideas will be derived from external and/or internal factors.
    External factors:
- Word-of-mouth: recommendations from friends and colleagues

- Media advertising: publicity material specifically designed to attract customers
- Previous visits to similar venues
- General impressions (derived often from television) about a range of facilities.

Internal factors:

- Gender: some activities are heavily influenced by gender, for whatever reason, e.g. aerobics and yoga tend to be female dominated, whereas boxing and windsurfing tend to be male dominated
- Age: some activities are very age-specific, e.g. skate-boarding at one end of the scale, and bowls at the other
- Education: some activities are stimulated by educational experiences and the desire to learn more, e.g. visits to art galleries and museums
- Culture: some activities are heavily influenced by 'collective culture' or 'subculture', often irrespective of education background, e.g. tennis clubs tend to have a rather middle/upper-class intake, whereas fishing clubs tend to attract a different sector of the population
- Life cycle: many activities are undertaken when one is part of a family, e.g. visits to the circus, trips to a theme park or fun-fair, but would not be undertaken alone, perhaps in later life. (In such cases, age may not be the only determinant therefore.)

Customer perceptions

Perception is not as simple a concept as it might seem, for several reasons:

1   Customers may assign a higher importance to certain parts of the experience (e.g. the ancillary facilities) than does the management.
2   Different customers may perceive the same experience quite differently from each other.
3   The same customer may view an experience differently from one visit to another, depending on his or her mood.
4   People often 'see what they want to see' – they may be determined to have a good time whatever the quality of the food, or may be determined to be miserable however great the show.

Generally speaking, the selectivity of the senses operate at both a conscious and unconscious level. At the conscious level, a person may concentrate on specific aspects of a site, at the relative exclusion of other features. At an unconscious level, the person will receive a 'general impression' which might represent the totality of the experience – or maybe one instance of poor treatment – either of which is sufficient to mould the final outcome.

External factors influencing perception will include the following:

- Movement – the human eye is attracted to moving images perhaps by instinct – thus it is difficult to ignore a 'live' television however hard one tries
- Repetition – thresholds of sensory perception are strongly influenced by repetition, and a stimulus which is often repeated, e.g. a television advert, is easier to recall than a single exposure
- Pattern – Gestalt psychology confirms that people tend to see patterns and connections as a means to aid recall, and that humans even create patterns – perhaps as a mechanism to understand their environment – even where it is obvious that none exists, e.g. signs of the zodiac
- Colour – people react to colour in ways which are often 'culturally determined', which is why, for example, adults associate the colour red with 'danger signs', whereas a child will be attracted to a piece of play equipment (or machinery!) which is bright red
- Contrast – sometimes the stimuli may be so conflicting as to reduce awareness, in which case it may be contrast (dark/light or noise/silence) which attracts the attention
- Novelty – a service or feature which is unique to one particular venue is easier to publicize and market than one which is common to all such venues
- Consistency – equally, a service needs to be consistent if it is to be provided at all – nothing is more annoying than vending machines which refuse to vend after taking the money!
- Association – those who visit specific leisure facilities often do so because these are 'associated' with something else, e.g. visiting a fitness centre, in the appropriate garb, may be associated with 'being fit' in itself.

Customer assessment

How do the customers remember their experience, and would the memory be sufficiently positive to encourage their repeat visit?

Whilst motivation, preconception and perception are all rather difficult to elicit and measure, it is much easier to establish how customers assess their experience, either:

- during and at the end of the visit, or
- at some predetermined time after the visit.

Customer appraisal carried out during the visit or at the visit-end can be done face to face, through a market interview process, or by questionnaire-type response, completed by the customer and left in a particular location. Face-to-face interviews are generally more successful in terms of their response rate, but there is a danger that the customer will give answers that the interviewer looks for, due to the nature of the questioning or the interviewer's body language.

Customer appraisals carried out after the visit have certain advantages, since the respondent may be less harassed and more able to take a more balanced view of what pleased and did not please during the visit. Questionnaires sent out, say, a week afterwards may be quite useful – provided that they are returned. Various incentives are used to encourage a 'return'. An alternative method is to use a telephone survey, which has the advantage of a greater response rate.

Encouraging repeat business

A person who is already present at a leisure venue is much easier to reach and to influence than someone who is 'out there'. Marketing is very expensive, after all, and it is sometimes said that persuading an existing customer to return is five times cheaper than finding a new one.

The following means to encourage repeat business can be considered:

- good 'first impressions', value for money, etc. from the initial visit
- membership schemes, e.g. offering priority bookings and/or social events or newsletters
- reduced charges for a 'series-booking' where applicable (often used for concerts)
- vouchers for a reduced 'second visit' admission charge
- vouchers for reduced charges at ancillary facilities, e.g. restaurant/crèche
- 'loyalty cards' – used extensively by supermarkets but could be used by larger commercial leisure companies
- bring-a-friend schemes – where both parties benefit through reduced prices
- publicity initiatives – sending out information, details of special offers etc. using a mailing list (postcodes also tell a great deal about customer catchment areas)
- special offers, e.g. discounted admissions charges during off-peak periods, to target groups.

If the policy is successful, and a high percentage level of repeat business established, then the manager can at least relax a little – knowing that the 'income base' is not quite so volatile as it might otherwise have been – and that expenditure on publicity is so much lower.

Managing contractors

In Chapter 2 we explained that all contracts are agreements, but not all agreements are contracts. Contracts are therefore particular types of agreement, their special nature underpinned by civil law.

The principles of contract management are as follows:

- Roles (client/contractor and contractor/subcontractor) must be understood and adhered to strictly.
- Any party to a contract must know what a contract represents, what is to be performed, and what the consequences of a 'breach' might be.
- Contracts between contractors and subcontractors are quite distinct from contracts between clients and contractors. It follows that clients should not give instructions to a subcontractor directly but only through the contractor, and only then with the latter's agreement.
- Great care must be exercised by managers who allow contractors into their buildings, e.g. for cleaning purposes or for maintenance. They should recognize that the public may not distinguish between such contractors and the venue's own staff. Whilst contractors are expected to use their professional knowledge in maintaining public safety, managers are none the less advised to ensure that due safeguards – physical barriers, warning signs etc. – are duly in place.
- Contractors, for their parts, need to understand the characteristics of the 'leisure environment', especially where the venue is still open to the public whilst work is in progress.

Generally speaking, the relationships between client and contractor will proceed smoothly provided that both parties understand the quality and quantity of their obligations.

Figure 4.2 illustrates 'who does what' within the client/contractor relationship, whilst Figure 4.3 sets out the various parts of a 'minor works' contract, in the form of a sequence-duration diagram (precisely as with those used for event-planning: see Chapter 6). The latter approach is vital if, for example, the manager wants to keep a part of the complex open to the public, whilst work is in progress. He or she would need to know which areas were being disrupted, and for how long.

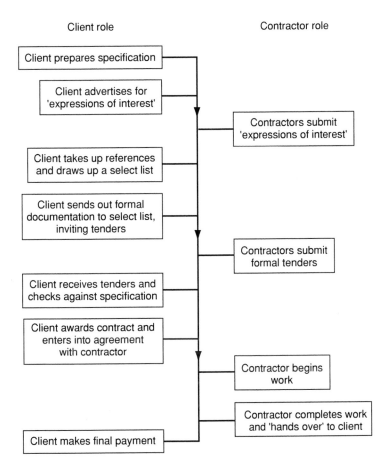

Client role   Contractor role

Figure 4.2 The tendering process for a medium/large contract

Similarly, where one job cannot begin until another ends, such a diagram can be used for planning purposes by the contractor, thereby ensuring that tasks are completed in the correct sequence, e.g. plastering before painting or decorating.

Client role

The client is expected to know what is required, and to have the money to pay the contractor – either upon completion of the contract or at intervals during the contract period ('stage payments').

A client is also expected to recognize the possibility of 'unforeseen problems' which the contractor may discover, and to approve any variation orders (i.e. variation to the original contract) where necessary.

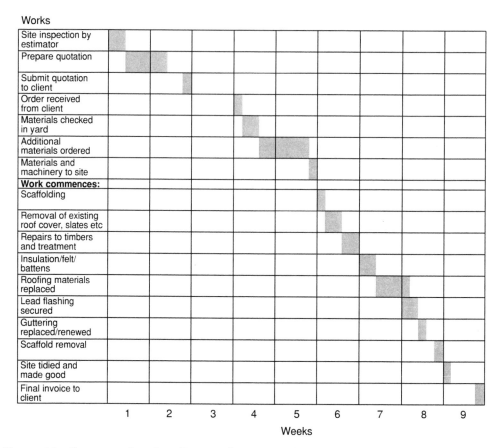

Figure 4.3 Sequence-duration diagram for a minor building contract (re-roofing)

Problems occur when a client is unclear as to what he or she wants – or, worse still, when a client has a change of mind (whether adding to contractor's work or reducing it) during the course of the contract. If a proper specification is prepared by the client – or someone acting on behalf of the client – then such problems will not occur.

Contractor role

A contractor is expected to perform the tasks which are set out in the contract itself plus relevant documents (e.g. specifications, tenders, bills of quantity, etc.).

Unless the client is advised to the contrary, the contractor will complete the 'work as described' (in the documentation) for the sum of money agreed.

Sometimes clients withhold a small percentage of the payment, in case faults subsequently arise, i.e. a 'retention sum'.

If the contractor is competent, well organized, and knows what the client expects, then all should go well. When a contractor is carrying out work while the public are within the vicinity, operational difficulties will almost certainly occur, e.g. vandalism, theft of equipment and tools. In general, problems are most acute when a contractor is building something such as a sports pavilion, on public open space, simply because the site is accessible at all times.

All in all, a good working relationship between client and contractor is essential, perhaps more so in the 'operational' world of leisure, where small or medium-scale companies have insufficient resources to carry out much work in-house. Certain works will always have to be 'contracted out' (e.g. specialist plant repairs, boiler inspection, electrical/gas installations, asbestos removal, etc.), whereas more modest tasks, carrying less risk or liability, can be handled internally.

Conclusions

Managing people is not an easy business: people may damage things, may behave unpredictably, and may even do things which endanger their own lives – or the lives of others. Staff too can be unpredictable, often basing their responses (to management initiatives, say) on their own cognitive reality. Managing staff then becomes a delicate balance between 'getting the job done' and 'keeping people happy'. Ultimately it is the task itself which must be afforded the higher priority, whereas ensuring staff motivation is a means to that end and not an end in itself.

Managing contractors is a very different matter because motivation is not at issue. Instead, reliability and competence on the contractor's part – plus a knowledge of what needs to be done, on the client's part – are necessary if the relationship is to be effective.

Having said all this, it is arguably the case that managing people can be a very gratifying experience. For most leisure managers it represents the best part of the job, even though the task can be frustrating.

References and recommended reading

Allport, G.W. (1965). *Letters from Jenny*. Harcourt Brace & World, New York.

Kohn, A. (1993). *Why incentive plans cannot work.* Harvard Business Review, September/October.

Martens, R. (1987). *Coaches Guide to Sports Psychology.* Springer-Verlag Inc., New York.

McKenna, E. (1994). *Business Psychology and Organizational Behaviour.* Lawrence Erlbaum Associates Ltd., Hove, East Sussex.

Milgram, S. (1965). *Some conditions of obedience and disobedience to authority. Human Relations,* 33, 369–382.

Rice, C. (1993). *Consumer Behaviour: Behavioural aspects of marketing.* Butterworth-Heinemann.

Rotter, J.B. (1954). *Social Learning and Clinical Psychology.* Prentice Hall, New York.

Thomas, K.W. (1976). *Conflict and conflict management.* In M. Dunnette (Ed), *Handbook of Industrial and Organizational Psychology.* Rand McNally.

5 Managing money

Questions

At the end of this chapter you should be able to undertake the following:

1 Identify how financial information may be used to assess the performance of a private sector company, a local authority leisure department and a local voluntary organization.
2 Examine the Annual Report of a large commercial leisure company, and indicate how the information contained in the report would be useful to (a) shareholders, (b) employees and (c) suppliers of goods and services (to the commercial company).
3 Discuss the reasons why a leisure manager needs to have an understanding of financial terminology, and a working knowledge of financial procedures.

Introduction

Although it helps for them to be reasonably adept at maths, students of leisure management need feel no anxiety at approaching this important topic. The key skills are not mathematical as such – except for an ability to divide, multiply, add and subtract – but rather:

- an understanding of financial concepts
- a familiarity with financial documentation
- an ability to think logically
- a capacity to scrutinize figures methodically
- an appreciation of double entry book-keeping, which requires only addition and subtraction. A trial balance is prepared periodically as a simple though not conclusive check on the completeness and accuracy of the entries.

Inevitably, the range of tasks that comes under the term 'financial responsibility' (on a Job Description for example) will be wide. Leisure managers may find that they are almost personally responsible, to a board of Trustees say, for a fairly modest budget. Alternatively, they may be part of a team with a collective responsibility for a much larger budget.

For the same reason any student of leisure management will find a distinct advantage in competing for jobs, if he or she possesses some financial knowledge – even where the opportunities to apply the knowledge in the form of a skill have been limited.

Simply to list the many texts on 'finance', and thereafter leave students to their own devices is not an alternative, in my view. Since the subject is so large and the material so voluminous, students are left floundering, with little guidance as to what matters and what does not (it is possible to study for a certificate in finance for the non-financial specialist).

This chapter will therefore try to indicate some basic principles of financial management, whilst accepting that further 'in-depth' reading, by students, will almost certainly be necessary.

The sequence of topics within the chapter is as follows:

1   Financial objectives, planning and management
2   Financial procedures and processes: budgets, cash flow, company accounts
3   Financial concepts: cost behaviour, break-even and depreciation
4   Assessing financial performance.

Financial objectives, planning and management

A private sector company will generally have clearer financial objectives than an organization in the public sector, though the latter will have limited objectives relating to specific operations. For example, a commercial company will seek to create fixed assets, or enhance the value of existing assets (e.g. by obtaining planning consent for a piece of land), neither of which concerns the public sector, where 'asset values' do not come into their accounting procedures, i.e. they do not produce balance sheets.

Voluntary bodies sometimes have clear objectives in relation to their future plans, e.g. a local athletics club needs to assemble resources for a new pavilion, the local amateur dramatic society for a new rehearsal/storage facility. Such bodies would look to 'money-making projects', and to grant-aid, rather than borrowing from the banks, with associated costs. Sports clubs tend to be quite single-minded in this type of enterprise, and often receive more help from sports councils and local authorities than do other groups.

Private-sector financial objectives

Something needs to be said about the objectives applied to private sector companies. They may be one of the following, or a combination of all three, i.e. different objectives and time scales for different segments of the operation:

- immediate return investment (within two years)
- medium-term return investment (within six years)
- long-term return investment (within ten years).

The period of return-investment depends partly upon the capital outlay, which itself depends upon the nature of the organization. A 'laser game' centre, for example, may hold its premises on a short lease, may hire its staff on fixed-term contracts but will have to pay for the laser equipment 'up-front'. Thereafter, it will run on minimum staffing levels, and while the activity remains popular, will expect to recoup its capital expenditure (on equipment), and make some reasonable profit, within the first two years. Provided its overheads (expenditure) are kept under control, and the customers are prepared to come along and pay the admission charge (income), then the business will flourish.

In addition, company financial objectives could be as follows:

- to 'corner the market', e.g. through retailing a novel service or product
- to 'corner the market' by squeezing out the opposition, e.g. through reducing prices and absorbing a temporary loss
- to secure a long-term financial base, whilst accepting short/medium-term losses (satellite television companies tend to work to this principle)
- to create a company which is 'asset-rich', even if annual profits (as shown by the profit and loss account) are quite modest
- to create a company which, although not 'asset-rich', has value by virtue of its total turnover (sales), or numbers of contracts won, etc. (leisure management companies fall into this category).

Rarely do companies have short-term objectives only – excepting the type of leisure management operation referred to earlier – but tend to have strategic medium and long-term plans.

Theoretically, the company should have six steps in mind:

1 Identify objectives clearly
2 Identify means to measure those objectives (the means are sometimes called 'performance indicators', e.g. a profit margin of X per cent)
3 Consider and define 'current position', e.g. in relation to assets purchased, liabilities entered into, profit thus far, etc.
4 Identify short/medium/long-term goals
5 Identify means to attain these goals
6 Review and evaluate, modifying objectives/performance indicators as necessary (i.e. a 'learning cycle').

Business plans

Business plans are essential documents: they show where the organization stands, financially speaking, and where it wishes to get to.

For the private sector, such plans help to convince potential lenders of capital that their 'investment' is in safe hands, and will be repaid with 'interest'; for the public sector, they represent forward-planning documents, especially for the Direct Service Organizations (DSOs) which sprang up as a result of CCT; for voluntary bodies, they are useful guidelines to plot the way forward, and will be of vital importance if any major capital schemes (e.g. a new pavilion or arts centre) are envisaged for the future.

Contents of a business plan

Given that most business plans are designed to convince potential lenders, or grant-givers, that the 'requesting organization' is a sound one, it seems reasonable that large financial institutions should advise applicants on how to prepare their documents. Similarly, advice is available from the National Lottery for potential applicants for lottery monies.

Barclays Bank, for example, provides a Business Plan Form which, as it explains, will help people to formulate their own business plans. The headings suggested are as follows:

- Introduction
- Details of the business
- Personal details (of those submitting the proposal)

- Personnel (cost of employing others, over first two years)
- Product/Service (descriptions, contributions to turnover, selling prices, costs)
- The Market (description, location, scale, growth-rate, competitors' prices, strengths and weaknesses, advantages of proposer's product or service over competitors, sales forecasts, rational for estimates)
- Marketing (marketing undertaken by competitors, marketing proposals, costs, source of estimates)
- Premises/Machinery/Vehicles (location, type and size of premises, lease/licence/rental details, machinery required, costs associated with machinery, lifespan of machinery)
- Record system (how records are to be prepared, and kept up to date)
- Objectives (personal short-term/medium-term, long-term objectives, how they are to be achieved)
- Finance (orders received, value and life expectancy of current assets, 'start-up' items and costs for first year, how paid for, creditors, available credit from suppliers, financial requirements, i.e. personal investment in the business, other security)
- Other (accountant, solicitor, VAT registration, insurance arrangements).

The document is very searching in its questions, and the questionnaire format makes completion easier. Any organization considering the preparation of a business plan would be advised to approach their own bank to see if similar guidelines are available. The Sports Council also provides some Guidance Notes on the production of business plans, but these are insufficient on their own.

Financial management

Money is a store of value, a measure of liability and a medium of exchange. But money is also transient, and has no fixed abode: it can flow in as income or can flow out as expenditure.

Money has to be managed, if it is to be used effectively to further the aims and objectives of the organization. And at its most basic, money needs to be 'brought in', if the organization is to be able to meet its bills.

Other reasons for financial management include the following:

- Private-sector companies are expected to make a profit (shareholders expect fairly immediate returns, more so in the United Kingdom than in some other economies), and financial management makes this possible.

- Public-sector organizations are expected to manage their budgets properly, to reduce their deficits/increase their income, to break even or make a small profit.
- Voluntary-sector organizations have to be careful to 'balance the books' if they are to ensure future survival.
- Money is a resource which can be transmuted into assets, e.g. by purchasing land, excepting that the asset may turn into a 'liability' if, say, the land turns out to be a former land-fill site.
- Money is a 'performance indicator' which has the advantage of being measurable and relevant.
- Organizations which handle money, i.e. all organizations, except for those dealing in barter-type systems (LETS for example), have a responsibility to creditors and to government, e.g. for VAT returns, corporation tax, reports to lenders, etc.
- When assets are converted back into money – a process sometimes described as 'going liquid' – through disposal, then the money can be used for other purposes, e.g. to pay debts (thus reducing liabilities) to buy raw materials, to buy finished goods, to build new premises.

In all, financial management is of fundamental importance if the organization has any expectation of success. Should company finances be mishandled, then bankruptcy will leave behind a trail of debts to other unfortunate companies and individuals.

Financial procedures and processes

Budgets

The idea behind the budgeting process is very simple – what makes it difficult are the larger numbers and the accounting procedures (i.e. the detail).

The purpose of a budget is to predict the movement of the money-resource, both inputs (income) and outputs (expenditure) over a given period, normally a 'financial year'. This period can be a calendar year, or may coincide with a 'tax year', or whatever dates are convenient to the organization.

Preparing a budget

Creating a realistic budget is as much an art as a science. The skill involves a combination of zero-based budgeting (all prediction) and a scrutiny of past performance, and of money-gone-by ('actuals'), to predict what might, or should, happen in the next accounting period.

Ideally, the person who is responsible for creating the budget should have access to the 'actuals' for at least two, and preferably three, preceding financial years. (Individuals, as well as companies, also consider their expenditure in relation to their income, though they rarely do so over a whole year, except when it comes to submitting a tax return.)

Exercise 5.1 Preparing a budget

Here is a simple exercise. Some headings are provided for you to put numbers against – more can be added, if you wish, or simply use the 'miscellaneous' category. This shows how to calculate your actual income and expenditure, for the year prior to reading this book. Where your weekly expenditure is stable e.g. £25 per week on travel, then simply multiply by 52; where expenditure is sporadic, you will have to 'estimate' what you spent during the year, e.g. on holidays. Total up your income, and your expenditure likewise. Where there is neither income nor expenditure for a heading, write 'nil' (see table on next page).

Something is missing, perhaps?

You may see certain problems emerging: most people, when they do such an exercise for the first time – and even after many attempts – discover that they end up with what should be a surplus, i.e. they should have money in the bank, building society or pocket, at the end of the year. But for the vast majority of cases, that surplus never appears.

Common problems with budgeting are as follows:

- People tend to under-estimate expenditure, forgetting the hundreds of smaller items which add up to a great amount.
- People indulge in selective perception, e.g. those who smoke 20 cigarettes a day will be reluctant to write the cost per day $\times$ 365, since the outcome will be almost £1000, i.e. the cost of a good holiday each year!
- Many new businesses are prone to over-estimate income: in their enthusiasm for the newly launched enterprise, they may forget the inhibiting factors which can so easily affect attendances.

Incidentally, you will perhaps have noticed that something quite important has been deliberately omitted from the expenditure column. Can you identify what it is? Clue: expenditure on the missing item would vary between £20 and £30 per week per person. (The answer of course is 'food'.)

Actual Income & Expenditure, year to date				
My Actual Income and Expenditure for the year ended (today)				
Income	£	*Expenditure*		£
Wages or salary (net after tax)		*Accommodation*	Rent	
Local authority grant			Mortgage	
Summer vacation job			Property repairs	
Christmas bonus			Insurance	
Other income (specify)		*Utilities*	Water	
			Gas	
			Electricity	
			Telephone	
		Transport (own)	Car loan repayment	
			Car repairs fund	
			Road fund licence	
			Car insurance	
			Running costs (petrol/oil)	
			Public transport	
		Holidays	Holiday cost	
			Travel insurance	
		Miscellaneous	Purchase of clothes	
			Laundry costs	
			Purchase of books and newspapers	
			Hospitality and entertainment	
Total income			**Total expenditure**	

Difference between Actual Income and Actual Expenditure
(brackets denote a deficit)

Budgetary estimates

Preparing a budget for the year-following is much easier, because there is something to 'go on', namely actual expenditure for the previous year. Try setting out your own budget, using the same format, for the next year. Try also to be more realistic: the chances are that your previous 'profit' – which was an illusion anyway – has now vanished, perhaps to be replaced by a small predicted loss.

The budget for the next year is calculated as follows:

- Assumptions are made about income, based on what is anticipated for the year.
- Calculations for expenditure headings can be made in line with inflation, for some items (e.g. food, utilities, petrol), may be left unchanged, or may even reduce (e.g. through obtaining a better deal on house-contents or car insurance). At one time, when inflation was running at 30 per cent per annum, accountants commonly used different 'indexes' (for wages, utilities, materials and such-like), but this method is less called for when inflation is very low.
- For large organizations, there may be 'segmented' budgets, e.g. one for the marketing department, one for production, one for buildings and estates, etc. Each departmental head, or 'budget-holder', will then be responsible for ensuring that no over-spend occurs, and also for reporting any significant reductions in anticipated income.

Where all the segmented budgets are drawn together, for the organization as a whole, this becomes what is sometimes called the 'master budget'.

Budgetary monitoring

Once the budget has received formal approval, there needs to be a mechanism put in place to monitor income and expenditure. In particular, attention needs to be paid to significant deviations that become apparent as the year progresses – delaying any scrutiny until the end of the financial year is of course too late. Most large organizations in any case prepare an 'anticipated out-turn' either half way or two-thirds of the way into their financial year.

Usually, under-expenditure is not a cause for concern, unless it represents 'delayed expenditure' (e.g. on maintenance) which might have more serious financial repercussions in the longer term. Under-expenditure may alternatively represent 'lost opportunity'. Over-expenditure is what normally worries the budget-holder, for unless that is a clear explanation for the excess or 'variance', and unless monies can be diverted from elsewhere within the approved budget (a process termed 'virement') then the matter is serious.

Budgetary monitoring is made easier through the use of spreadsheets, where the computer prints out financial data in column form, usually month by month. One column would normally show 'expenditure-to-date'; another 'commitments' (e.g. orders made by an organization to a supplier of goods or services); another the total of both. A fourth column may show what should have been spent thus far, according to whether the expenditure is regular or cyclical, and a fifth column the difference between the 'theoretical expenditure' and the 'actual-plus-commitments'·expenditure. This last column indicates effectively, how the budget is faring, and should give the degree of 'variance'. Variance represents the difference between what was predicted in the budget, and what is actually happening, expressed as either a percentage or figure.

What steps can be taken if the spreadsheet indicates an overspend? The options open to the budget holder are as follows:

- Put an immediate block on any further expenditure from this budget heading or expenditure code, until the matter has been investigated.
- Arrange for a 'virement' or transfer to be made from one expenditure code to another, subject to any financial regulations which may apply.
- Consider whether any additional income might be forthcoming – this would not excuse over-expenditure, but might make the 'reporting session' less painful.

For those who find it difficult to spot significant variances through horizontal scanning of the figures in their respective columns, an option is to translate the data into purely visual form using bar charts or line graphs.

Cash flow

Control of cash flow – monies coming in and out – is extremely important for several reasons. Many firms 'go under' even when their budgets appear reasonable, simply because they do not receive sufficient payment (from large purchasers of their goods, for example) and therefore cannot pay their staff or meet other crucial items of expenditure, e.g. loan repayments. If all else fails, the 'creditors', from whom they borrowed money, may call in the Official Receiver, and the company must cease trading. 'Trading while knowingly insolvent' is an offence in the United Kingdom.

Cash-flow management is vital for the following reasons:

- Many items of expenditure must be paid almost immediately when demanded, e.g. salaries, and cannot be delayed until 'more income arrives'.

- Cash-flow monitoring allows for the scrutineer to detect small trend-changes over shorter periods, which if left uncorrected would cause major distortions to the final out-turn.

Cash-flow monitoring is normally conducted on a month-by-month schedule, though large companies might use the week-by-week approach.

Where the operation of an organization has a seasonal pattern to its income, i.e. most leisure facilities, then cash-flow monitoring becomes yet more important. Operations which are primarily 'outdoor' in the United Kingdom (fun-fairs, zoos, theme parks, outdoor pools) experience substantial reductions in their income during the winter months – but they still carry various fixed costs, and have staff to employ, grounds to maintain, buildings to repair, utility bills to pay, if they are to continue in existence until the next season. Sadly, an 'expenditure-free period' is not possible, though an 'income-less' one is. The same is true for individuals, of course ...

As with budgets, so with cash flow: the best way to understand is not to read, but to do. If it would help, therefore, try this exercise.

Exercise 5.2 Cash-flow forecasting

Month-before-last:

Consider your income and expenditure for the last two months, and complete the right-hand column, headed Actual. Leave the Forecast column as it is, because in this instance someone has done the forecast for you.

Try to calculate both income and expenditure as accurately as possible, when completing the Actual column. Some of the expenditure figures can be calculated by dividing the annual sums in Exercise 5.1 by 52. Then calculate your Closing Bank Balance in the same way as has been done for the Forecast. Note that your Closing Bank Balance for the month-before-last becomes your Opening Bank Balance for the last month. The same principle applies throughout the process.

Now assess how different are your Actuals from what was forecast: the difference is called 'variance'.

Last month:

Using the same format and basing your figures upon the last Actuals, calculate a Forecast for what you should have spent and received last month. The chances are that you will have guessed your income reasonably well, but have underestimated your expenditure.

In theory, you could prepare such a cash-flow chart for a complete financial year (i.e. 12 charts in all) and by this means ensure that you have sufficient monies to pay your most pressing bills.

Cash-flow forecast

	Month before last Forecast	Actual	Last month Forecast	Actual
Receipts	£	£	£	£
Wages/Salary	150			
Grant	250			
Other receipts	135			
Total receipts (A)	535			
Payments				
Transport	25			
Food	75			
Fees	100			
Entertainment	50			
Books & Newspapers	25			
Rents/leases	200			
Utilities	40			
Other	65			
Total payments (B)	580			
Opening bank balance	NIL		(45)	
Add total receipts (A)	535			
Less total payments (B)	580			
Closing bank balance	(45)			

*Figures in brackets denote a deficit

Cash-flow forecasting allows an organization to:

- make immediate changes to expenditure if income falls dramatically
- relate monies in/out to the annual budget (since the totals for predicted income and predicted expenditure should be the same for cash-flow forecast and budget after adjustment for creditors and pre-payment, e.g. telephone rental)

- ensure that 'lean-periods' of reduced income are anticipated in such a way as to allow for unavoidable expenditure, e.g. on salaries. This is particularly important, given the 'seasonality' factor which affects both leisure and tourism.

Company accounts

Private sector companies normally produce their accounts according to guidelines or rules established by the following means:

1 Acts of Parliament/State legislatures, e.g. The Companies Acts 1985.
2 Professional requirements/accounting standards laid down in the United Kingdom by such bodies as the Institute of Chartered Accountants, the Chartered Association of Certified Accountants or the Chartered Institute of Public Finance and Accountancy.
3 Procedural rules drawn up by the 'money markets', e.g. listing rules of the Stock Exchange.

Company accounts appear in three characteristic formats, namely:

- trading accounts
- profit and loss accounts
- balance sheets.

The first two are generally shown together in a simple document. The title 'profit and loss accounts' is replaced by 'income and expenditure statement' for entities that are not businesses.

All accounts are kept on 'double entry' principles which means that each 'credit' entry has an equal and opposite 'debit' entry and vice versa. Often the leisure manager only makes single entries of cash and the double entry is made by accounting staff.

Trading accounts

A trading account shows the basic relationship between what a company receives in the form of 'sales' and what it spends when buying in the goods it sells ('cost of goods sold'). The trading account will show the 'purchases' during the year, and will incorporate the expenditure made on the 'opening stock', since the income from selling that stock is within the sales figure for the year. By contrast, the 'closing stock' is excluded from the calculation, since even though the goods may have been paid for, any income derived from selling that stock will not appear until the next financial year. At the end of the trading account is a balance which is known as the gross profit/loss.

Profit and loss accounts

Profit and loss accounts are more straightforward, in that they show the 'expenditure' picture more fully, by setting these against the gross profit referred to earlier. The balance shown by the Profit and Loss Account, combined with a trading account, is called the net profit/loss.

These accounts are prepared on the 'accruals concept' where for example the amount customers have not yet paid for goods supplied is shown in the balance sheet as a current asset and the amount owed to suppliers is shown in the balance sheet as a current liability.

Example of a trading and profit and loss account

Most leisure venues incorporate bars within their confines. The drinks which are sold at these bars represent the 'sales' (income) for the year. The 'cost of goods sold' is the expenditure which the venue makes in paying the brewery for the purchase of those drinks ('wastage', a problem in all bars, will be accounted for when unsold items purchased do not appear in the closing stock). There will be other expenses, of course, such as staff costs, cleaning and refurbishment. Depreciation of furniture/fittings may also be included as an item of expenditure (this concept will be explained later).

Thus a simple set of accounts for the year ended _____

	£	£
Sales		170 000
Less: Cost of goods sold		
Opening Stock	25 000	
Purchases	90 000	
	115 000	
Less: Closing Stock	20 000	95 000
Gross Profit		75 000

Expenses		
Staff cost	23 000	
Cleaning	6 000	
Utilities	3 000	
Depreciation	4 000	
Maintenance	1 000	
Total expenses	_____	37 000
Net Profit for the period		38 000

No taxation is shown within these simplified accounts: in reality, these will be net profit 'before' and 'after' taxation. Were this a separate company, the latter figure would, in effect, be available for:

1 distribution to shareholders (in the form of dividends) or
2 putting into 'reserves' or
3 identified as 'retained profit for the year'.

If the entity is registered for value added tax (VAT), no VAT is included in the figures, but the current amounts must be accounted for to the United Kingdom customs and excise authorities. If the entity is not registered for VAT, no VAT is added to value but VAT paid out is included in expenditure.

Balance sheets

A balance sheet represents the snapshot of a company at a point of time, by showing the assets (fixed and current) which it possesses, as against the liabilities (long term/short term) which it carries.

A company may be 'asset rich' for example, but show a rather poor trading picture in its trading and profit and loss accounts. Another company could show a healthy net profit but have virtually no fixed assets such as factories or offices.

In showing the relationship between assets and liabilities, the balance sheet demonstrates the ability of the company to pay its outstanding creditors, if the need were to arise. The 'proximity to cash' (liquidity) is the crucial measure in this instance.

Preparing a company's balance sheets requires considerable expertise, and is an unlikely task for the average leisure manager. None the less, the basic formula is worth mentioning, since it explains why a balance sheet is laid out in a specific way, and why, in fact, it is intended to 'balance'. The most common formula is:

FA + (CA–CL) = C + LTL

an alternative being:

FA + CA = C + LTL + CL

where FA represents fixed assets, CA current assets, LTL long-term liabilities, CL current liabilities and C capital. 'Capital' represents the interest of the owners and constitutes the original introduction of funds by the owners and the performance thereafter.

'Capital' as shown in a balance sheet must never be confused with what a business may be purchased or sold for.

Financial concepts

Cost behaviour

Some costs are seen to rise (or fall) according to the level of customers or units of production. In a leisure centre for example, the bill for repairs to lockers would be substantial if usage escalated rapidly, whereas if no-one came the bill would be significantly less. Such costs are called 'variable costs'.

Other costs remain in place regardless of the number of customers or the units of production, and thus these are termed 'fixed costs'. Fixed costs are frequently related to (permanent) staff, and to other aspects of administration which are necessary whatever the output.

The third type of cost is called a 'mixed cost', and occurs when a particular item of expenditure contains both of the characteristics referred to above, i.e. some aspects are variable and others fixed. Such a cost occurs, for example, where a manager is on a set salary per month (a fixed cost) but also has a monthly bonus (a variable cost, according to output) – in which case the 'salary cost as a whole' is 'mixed' in behaviour. When mixed costs incorporate specific thresholds, the resultant figures are referred to as 'stepped costs'.

'Break even'

The concept of 'breaking-even', used in everyday speech, requires proper definition. Understanding the concept fully does require an understanding of cost behaviour, discussed earlier, plus some appreciation of the difference between absorption and marginal costing.

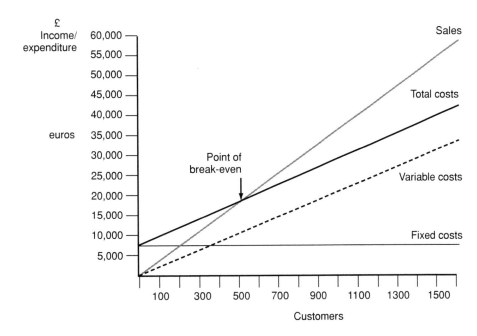

Figure 5.1 A break-even chart

The former refers to a system whereby costs are 'absorbed' by either the end product or the cost centres which comprise the business. Marginal costing is used when the fixed costs are allocated in total against the output, whereas the variable costs can be set against specifically that output.

In simple terms, a break-even point is reached when sales income matches total costs. Total costs are represented by fixed costs plus variable costs.

Figure 5.1 explains how useful a break-even chart might be, since it can:

- demonstrate the relationship between the company's fixed and variable costs
- show the point of break-even, after which the company may be said to operate at a profit ('the margin of safety')
- provide an indication of when, in terms of the X or Y axis parameters, the break-even point should occur. In effect, either parameter can become a 'target'.

Exercise 5.3

Using the chart provided, consider the following questions:

1 How much sales income can you expect from 1000 customers?

2   If you have a sales income of 50 000 euros how many customers does that represent?
3   What is the variable cost per customer?
4   If the variable cost per customer rises, what effect does this have upon the fixed costs?
5   If the fixed costs rise, what effect does this have upon total costs?

(Answers: 1. approx. 36 000 euros; 2. approx. 1400 customers; 3. approx. 20 euros per customer; 4. none; 5. they rise accordingly.)

Depreciation

Like so many financial notions, depreciation is quite simple: it refers to a process by which an asset is used up by the business and/or declines in value, over a period of time. We all recognize that certain assets go down in value, quite relentlessly, e.g. motor cars, whereas others tend to rise in value, e.g. houses. Under the prudence concept ('underestimate income and overestimate expenditure'), Trading and Profit and Loss accounts must include this loss in value but not the increase in value as this is not yet earned.

Ultimately, the value of a house or car will depend upon what someone is prepared to pay for it, irrespective of what an expert valuer says that it is worth, i.e. estate agent or garage.

Two methods of calculating depreciation are available:

1   Reducing-balance method – whereby the asset value is reduced by a fixed percentage each year, thus suffering a greater decline when it is at its greatest value (like a car) than in subsequent years.
2   Straight-line method. The straight-line approach is more 'accountancy-led', because it evens out the depreciation across the whole life of the asset, showing depreciation as an equal amount each year.

The main advantage of the second approach is its simplicity. Though it seems to defy common sense – for we know that new things usually depreciate faster than old ones – the technique works perfectly well if the asset is retained for the whole of its life.

The method of calculating straight-line depreciation is:

$$\frac{C - S}{N}$$

where C represents the original cost of the asset, S its residual ('book') value, and N the estimated life of the asset.

Wasting assets will need to be assessed at the end of every year – for example to assess the amount of reserves left in a quarry or the useable space left in a land-fill site.

Assessing financial performance

Because money is easily measurable, it is often used to assess the performance of an organization or venue. This is not to say that money is the only criterion of success, but that financial assessment is an important tool in any performance appraisal.

All too often, managers use words like 'profit' or 'break-even' or 'value for money' or 'efficiency' without knowing the true meaning. Where students use these words, however, they should ensure correct usage, in relevant contexts.

As with companies generally, commercial leisure organizations may be assessed by reference to their trading and profit and loss accounts, plus their balance sheets. Local authorities may be assessed through their published accounts, where the format is also standardized but is different from company accounts. Voluntary bodies may be assessed through their Annual Accounts, normally presented and ratified at their annual general meeting.

Financial ratios

Ratios, according to Dyson (1997), represent an attempt to relate one item to another, with the relationship between the two expressed as a percentage. The ratios which are commonly used fall into four broad headings, being for:

- profitability
- liquidity
- efficiency
- investment.

Ratio analysis is a useful tool for examining company accounts, but has less relevance for examining the financial performance of public (or voluntary) sector organizations.

Trend analysis

As its name suggests, trend analysis requires that specific items be scrutinized over a period of time. If one has expenditure details for five financial years, for example, it is possible to allocate a weighting of 100 to the first set of accounts and to express subsequent figures as a proportion of that initial starting point.

Horizontal analysis

Horizontal analysis is similar to trend analysis, except that figures are taken year-on-year, not reduced to a common base. The expenditure (or income) each year is expressed as a percentage of the year which precedes it.

Vertical analysis

Vertical analysis requires that individual items of expenditure be expressed as a percentage of the total expenditure of which they are a part. By this means, the performance of the individual item, in relative terms, can be considered over several financial years. Since it is the percentage which is relevant – and not the figure – one can more easily assess 'significance'.

Some organizations also make use of a performance audit, whereby their part or the whole organization is studied by external consultants. Like a safety audit, the performance audit can be a valuable means to spot problems and take remedial measures.

Utility audits are also used, whereby gas, water, and electricity boards will conduct surveys, for a modest cost, to check on the efficiency of particular installations. Similar surveys can be commissioned from specialist consultants.

Conclusions

Managing money is one of the most important skills in any management role. Unlike 'people skills', financial skills are not a matter of intuition – though intuition does play a part – but rather of understanding the various procedures, definitions and protocols which are used by the accountancy profession.

A leisure manager who understands finance has an enormous advantage over others, especially when it comes to defending the empire against the depredations of other departments. Understanding cost accounting procedures also helps, since the leisure manager may see how 'central' costs are 'absorbed' by departments such as his or her own.

In such circumstances as this, budgetary cuts would otherwise fall to the service (rather than the central) department, since the accounts may suggest that the latter costs nothing at all! CIPFA has traditionally written local government accounts using this particular form of subterfuge, i.e. making central services 'invisible', thus protecting the position of its members.

Pricing policy can also be easier if the leisure manager has a ready grasp of the figures. Because the options are so considerable and the decisions often influenced by non-financial considerations, the topic of pricing has not been addressed by this text. None the less it can be seen that from a policy standpoint, managers should appreciate the full extent of their expenditure before trying to set charges which, they hope, will be transmuted into income.

Whether the subject of finance has become clearer is for the reader to decide, but if the reading list looks at all appealing, then something has been achieved.

References and recommended reading

Dyson, J.R. (1997). *Accounting for Non-Accounting Students*. (4th edn). Pitman.
Gautier, M. and Underdown, B. (1993). *Accounting Theory and Practice*. Pitman.
Pendlebury, M. & Groves, R. (1990). *Company Accounts*. Unwin & Hyman.
Pizzey, A. (1989). *Accounting and Finance: A firm foundation*. Holt Reinhart Winston.
Underdown, B. and Taylor, P.J. (1985). *Accounting Theory and Policy Making*. Heinemann.

6 Managing programmes and events

Questions

At the end of this chapter you should be able to undertake the following:

1 Using the 'corporate model', set out the stages which would be required to promote a large firework display, within the confines of a public park, indicating also the permissions, licences and insurances which should be sought.
2 Suggest what might be the components of a successful event, and how these might be evaluated against the objectives of that event.
3 Identify the main differences between promoting events held outdoors and those held within enclosed venues.

Introduction

For our purposes, an event represents a 'unique occasion', which stands out from the normal course of an organization's work. A programme is more a series of occurrences or opportunities which, taken together, represent a coherent whole.

The distinction is purely pragmatic, and in reality there are many organizations which promote events on a regular basis across a specific period of time. Are these 'on–off' events, or is this a programme?

The principles of organization and marketing apply equally to both programmes and events, except that the former rely on a consistency of provision, whereas the latter may not.

Torkildsen (1983) initially saw the programme as the essence of recreation services, being the result of a process designed to meet the different needs of the community. He also argued that, while many organizations were involved in recreation programming, e.g. education authorities, religious organizations, the actual coordination should be carried out by local government. In this connection, he affirmed, local authorities have three roles, namely:

1   provision of facilities
2   coordination of resources combined with an 'enabling function'
3   management and leadership.

This approach, with its emphasis upon local authorities, has perhaps been overtaken by national politics, the diminution in their 'leisure role' by compulsory competitive tendering (CCT).

None the less, the idea of 'programming by objectives' remains as important now as it was then. Before the introduction of CCT, there was far less talk of 'objectives', 'performance indicators' and even of 'policies' than there was in the 1990s – at least within the realms of local government.

Again, a programme, as Torkildsen points out, may need to be seen as 'balanced', serving various user groups at a leisure centre, for example, whereas single events will have a different rationale. Indeed, programmes often reflect these different pressures to the point where they lose any individuality whatever, and become 'just another programme' at the local venue.

Before looking at the planning and managerial process, we need to say something about the relationship between venues, and programming.

Venues

Indoor venues

The following aspects must be considered:

- Physical suitability of the venue, in terms of its dimensions and layout.
- Financial suitability, in terms of its audience capacity, and hiring cost.
- Operational suitability, in terms of its resources, security and managerial expertise.
- Environmental suitability, in terms of any noise or nuisance which might otherwise be caused to the locality.
- Legal suitability, in terms of any permissions or licences which may be required.

Outdoor venues

Outdoor venues can be assessed in the same way as above, but in addition the following must be considered:

* Availability of an alternative indoor venue, should it become necessary, and subject to scale.
* Provision of resources which need to be hired well in advance, e.g. toilets, marquees, catering facilities.
* Liaison with statutory authorities in respect of traffic flows, on-street parking, emergency access onto the site (for ambulances, fire vehicles), site security and public safety.
* Greater emphasis on security of goods, money, and equipment, plus need for contingency planning and constant liaison between responsible bodies.
* Case for resources which are not required for indoor venues, e.g. first-aid marquee, 'lost children's collection point', mobile refreshments, wet weather cover of participants, where appropriate, if not for audience.
* Policy on cancellation due to weather needs to be clearly formulated and made explicit, so as to avoid any subsequent misunderstanding or bad feelings.

Managerial aspects of programming

Generally speaking, the management of a venue or facility will be responsible for the devising and marketing of a programme. Managers will know their physical and staff resources in detail, and will appreciate what the venue can best handle. Likewise, they will know its limitations.

Their task is to match their programme to the needs of the catchment which they serve, whether this is defined geographically or socially. Political pressures within a local authority will often lead to problems of 'balance', as has already been intimated, and subtle pressures will come from established clubs and societies which see themselves as having priority over newly created associations. Under circumstances of this nature, initiating a new organization, and finding space, can be very difficult.

Membership schemes also cause problems where programming is concerned, because members may have been promised times and dates for elements of a programme. The contractual relationship between 'member' and 'venue' may reduce the management's freedom to change the balance of a programme, should overall demand levels make this necessary or new groups require accommodation.

If events are seen as 'happening outside the normal run of things', advantage of managerial familiarity with the venue may not be pre instances, for example when an outside promoter hires a venue for a ro In-house promotions, by the venue management itself, are therefore more straight-forward than are 'external promotions' by a third party, handled either on the basis of 'straight hire' (i.e. for an agreed fee) or 'percentage split of box office (e.g. 50 per cent to venue and 50 per cent to promoter).

At some venues, the distinction between 'in-house' and 'external' promoters may become muddled, where for instance one particular promoter has used the venue for many years. If things go wrong, however, the matter can become complicated, and recourse to the terms of a contract unavoidable. Assuming that there is indeed a contract, it may be either of the following:

- the contract between promoter and artists/artists
- the contract between the promoter and the venue.

Where the promoter is external, both contracts will exist, whereas only the first will apply where the promoter is the venue management itself (the subject of contract law was examined briefly in Chapter 2).

Assessing demand

Assessing demand for programmes is often a very subtle matter, as managers will be aware. Internal pressures, based on 'pet ideas' from senior management, may play their part, as will external pressures from established groups which have used the venue for a long time.

The 'balancing act' referred to earlier, implies that the manager has to appease various interest groups, some internal but most external, e.g. between members and non-members, between one sport and another, between collective activities and more individualistic ones, and so forth. Where the organization's primary objective is to make a profit, this balancing act is inevitably tilted towards maximizing both primary and secondary income.

Assessing demand for a specific programme, or for amendments to an existing programme, can be achieved through the following means:

- Internal evaluation:
    meeting with staff to seek ideas
    meeting with representatives of existing users

questionnaires to all members, where a membership scheme operates
selective interviews of specific users
random interviews, e.g. at peak or off-peak times.
- External evaluation:
sample survey within locality, to ascertain needs of 'non-users'
specific actions to assess demand through new programmes, i.e. by trial and error
application of 'demand assessment' by matching national statistics (for participation in leisure activities) to the demographic and social characteristics of the locality (in this context, it is to be noted that the 'National Standard' yardstick, for such facilities as swimming pools, and sports centres is now rarely used as the sole methodology).

Assessing the demand for an event is much more a matter of 'intuition plus experience' on the part of the promoter, and unlike a programme, the financial out-turn cannot be improved half way through!

Entertainment managers in particular will sense what succeeds and what does not, as will commercial promoters who hire the venue for their event. A 'mixed programme' in this particular context, will involve both:

- 'direct promotions', whereby a contract exists between management and artiste, the former operating within an overall budgetary framework
- 'third-party promotions' by external promoters, operating within a contractual framework referred to earlier.

In the latter instance, management needs to be entirely clear on the legal basis of their 'hiring conditions', and should periodically check these to ensure compliance with current practices and regulations. Such conditions should naturally be explicit, in written form, and should be signed/dated by the hirer before the booking of the venue is confirmed. Similarly, any 'percentage split' of box office or any other income (e.g. for refreshment sales) must be agreed in writing either as part of the hiring agreement or as a separate contractual commitment. It is then a matter for the external promoter to sign a contract with the artiste(s), as this is not within the venue manager's remit.

The process of programme and event management

Accepting the previously mentioned differences between programmes and events, it still remains a fact that the similarities of organization are greater than the differences – which is why, in this chapter, we shall be considering the two together.

The chronological sequence which comprises the process may be summarized in various ways: for example, the Croner text (1992) refers to four stages, namely:

Phase 1.   Initial idea and feasibility
Phase 2.   Establishing organizational framework
Phase 3.   Detailed planning
Phase 4.   Post-event evaluation and procedures.

An alternative approach is also sequential but perhaps easier to remember, though more detailed. Some events are promoted by individuals working virtually alone, though most are run corporately – either by some form of 'collective enterprise' or by a 'voluntary committee'.

That being so, the nature of the process can be set out as in Table 6.1.

Table 6.1   Stages in programme and event promotion

Stage	Tasks
1 Conceptualization	Idea formulated and tested against one's own experience or the experience of other people.
2 Objective-setting	Objectives clearly established, and means to measure success or otherwise ('performance indicators') also formulated.
3 Resource-identifying	Physical and human resources, needed to promote the programme or event, clearly identified; preliminary financial resources (i.e. draft budget) also established.
4 Planning	Planning process begins, and permissions/licences sought, once any liaison with statutory authorities or landowners is completed.
5 Organization	Details are discussed and concluded; resources are hired where necessary and artistes contracted; venue is confirmed.
6 Refining	Adjustments may be needed to programme/event marketing, in light of advance ticket sales; all contracts finalized and arrangements checked.
7 Acquainting	The 'marketing push' which acquaints potential customers is most important at this stage, since a well-organized programme or event which no one attends cannot be considered a success.
8 'Turn out'	The event itself should appear professionally presented, should constitute what was promised in the publicity, should run to time, and should attract a maximum audience.
9 Evaluation	The programme or event should be evaluated against its objectives, using the performance indicators, and conclusions reached. These may form the 'feedback loop' if a repeat exercise is being contemplated.

No special claim is made for this nine-stage approach, except that perhaps the 'corporate acronym' should assist recall. Looking at each of the stages individually may also make things clearer.

Stage 1: Conceptualization

Some person or group will express an idea that 'such-and-such' might be worth trying. The concept will be refined, either informally after discussions with other bodies, or formally through a feasibility study.

A large-scale programme or event will probably mean that such a study is required, to convince those who control the purse-strings that an appropriate budgetary allocation should be made available. Thus, the feasibility study would incorporate some of the following:

- nature of the event
- aims and objectives
- human and equipment resources needed
- potential income
- potential expenditure
- potential problems to be overcome, e.g. permissions, licences, objections from within and without the organization
- potential benefits
- time scale required for organization.

Stage 2: Objective-setting

Programmes and events may have a single purpose behind them, or may represent the culmination of a series of worthy aspirations. Either way, objectives should be made explicit, and should not remain obscure or, worse still, conflicting. For example, if my first objective is to 'make an immediate profit' this may be at odds with my second objective which is to 'encourage the use of a facility by disadvantaged groups or individuals', where the latter necessitates my introducing cut-price admission charges.

Objectives may include one or more of the following:

- to make an immediate profit/break even, on the basis that income exceeds or matches expenditure

- to establish longer term profitability, by establishing and/or occupying a particular 'market niche'
- to eradicate the competition, e.g. by providing a better service for the same price as the competition, or by temporarily reducing charges for admission or participation ('special offers') so as to squeeze the opposition out of the picture
- to 'satisfy the needs of the local community'. As has been commented elsewhere, this type of objective was quite often seen within local authority-run leisure facilities before the introduction of CCT. However laudable it may seen, it is very difficult to measure such needs with any certainty, and impossible to meet every expressed need by providing the necessary resources
- to satisfy the needs of a particular cohort. This objective can be used to underpin GP referral schemes, for example, where the cohort represents people in poor health. An age-cohort could be 'over 65s', for instance, or 'teenagers' or 'under-fives'
- to improve the condition of disadvantaged groups, as part of the process of 'social amelioration', in a rural but more often an urban context. (Many leisure centres were constructed in inner-city areas of the United Kingdom during the 1970s and 1980s on the basis of this rationale.) Clearly, the list of those who are disadvantaged can be devised in such a way that virtually no-one is excluded – in which case there is no value in adopting such an objective in the first place!
- to encourage participation in a particular activity, or group of activities, so as to stimulate 'demand'. This is not quite the same as 'social amelioration', since it might represent a 'means-to-an-end' rather than an 'end' in itself. Thus, the real objective may be 'maximum take-up of space', and the stated objective becomes the means to that end.

However difficult it may seem, the organization promoting the programme or event should separate 'means' from 'ends' so that the two do not become muddled up. Obviously some objectives, such as 'to eradicate the opposition and thereby create a monopoly', cannot be included in the organization's 'mission statement', but most objectives can be set down and performance duly assessed.

Measuring performance

At the same time as objectives are established, the means to measure success should also be identified. If, for example, my objective is a 'make profit of X per cent of turnover', then this is easily measured once final accounts are to hand. The objective has either been met or it has not, and the 'performance indicator' is a matter of objective fact and not subjective opinion.

In brief, performance criteria for programmes/events should be as follows:

1   Explicit and measurable
2   Succinct and easy to understand
3   Objective where appropriate (e.g. using numbers of people, or amounts of money)
4   Subjective where appropriate (e.g. using customer opinion surveys as to the benefit received from visiting the venue)
5   Relevant to the objectives.

Stage 3: Resource-identifying

Resources will include some of the following:

*   Physical resources:
        land, e.g. for event-staging, car parking, access
        buildings, e.g. for main programme/event, plus ancillary facilities
        equipment, e.g. for particular activities within the programme
        seating, e.g. for spectator events
        staging, e.g. for dramatic productions
        security, e.g. fencing around site for certain outdoor shows
        facilities as per the specification required to accommodate the programme or event.
*   Organizational resources:
        individuals able to make the necessary time commitment
        individuals with the appropriate expertise
        support within the organization as a whole, e.g. where resources are needed at short notice.
    Legal resources:
        permissions from landowners or highway authorities where appropriate
        licences from magistrates court (liquor) or local authorities (PEL) or copyright licences, as applicable
        insurance company willing to provide 'cover'.
*   Financial resources:
        budget for items of expenditure
        authority and procedure for making payments to contractors/artistes

means to safeguard cash, where appropriate, e.g. for outdoor events
means to supervise income collection and arrange banking.

The complementary approach is that of the 'checklist', and indeed this is used in the Croner text. A checklist is extremely useful as an aid to identify resources which might otherwise be overlooked.

A distinct advantage can also be gained by combining the checklist with a sequence-time diagram, except that the 'alphabetical sequence' should be replaced by chronological sequence. Figure 6.1 demonstrates how very useful this exercise can be, even for the organizing of a relatively small event.

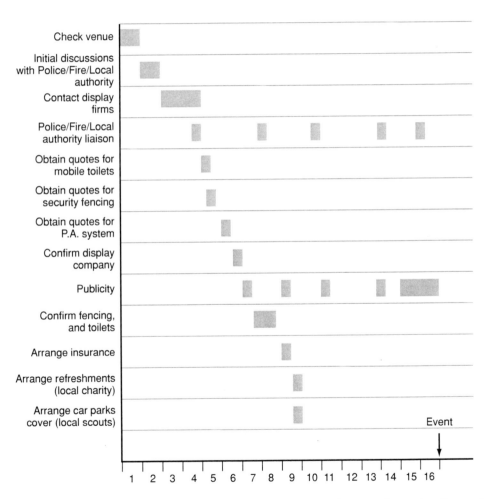

Figure 6.1 Sequence-duration diagram for a medium-scale event (town bonfire and firework display)

Stage 4: Planning

The planning phase presupposes that the idea has been elaborated, objectives agreed and resources identified, as well as costed. By this time, the organization will know whether or not it has the desire and the capability to proceed. It will also have agreed the mechanisms by which the project will be carried to fruition.

Individual and corporate mechanisms

Some events are promoted by individuals acting almost alone: they decide on the 'act', choose a venue, hire the venue, handle marketing and so forth. Such entrepreneurs would eschew a committee to which they would have to report as being a hindrance to decision making and a waste of time. Promoters who operate separately or through their own small company are, quite literally, 'free agents' albeit that they have to operate within the confines of contract law, employment law, and licensing law.

Other events are promoted ostensibly by an organization, whether public, private or voluntary. The programme or event carries their name and possibly those of any sponsors. In such circumstances, the organizers of the programme or event are not 'free individuals' but employees of an organization, and as such they must:

1   work within the organizational framework
2   follow procedures (e.g. financial regulations) which apply within the organization
3   use human and other resources which the organization decides to make available.

Where the 'corporate exercise' represents a scenario of this nature, the organizing committee is normally an ad hoc group, composed almost entirely of professional colleagues from within the organization.

A second 'corporate model' may be seen in contexts which are perhaps more 'social' or 'political' than purely commercial. For example, a local community centre may wish to promote a 'fun day' for the locality. To do this, the person responsible for running the centre (often an employee of a local authority) may establish a steering group of interested persons, e.g. a local shopkeeper, an enthusiastic sportsperson, a local representative of the district arts association, a local artist, and so on. The 'steering committee' becomes the 'planning committee' if and when the project appears feasible.

A community-corporate model such as that described above is quite different from the organizational-corporate model referred to earlier: its legal status is less defined, its powers less circumscribed by internal rules, its resources limited to what it can beg or borrow. Like the organizational model, however, this committee may be ad hoc, existing purely for the purpose of organizing the event, and not otherwise.

Corporate models of both sorts tend to select individuals who have particular expertise, and sometimes ambitions. Clearly, in the 'organizational-corporate model', the committee structure will be influenced by work roles, whereas the alternative model establishes its own roles and responsibilities, according to the task in hand. Organizational-corporate committees will not require a 'constitution', as such, and need have no distinction between 'lay members' (representing the 'community') and 'paid members' or 'officers'.

Community-based programmes and events are often promoted through the second type of corporate structure, but here again roles may vary according to the respective 'power base', since some of the committee members will be representatives of local clubs and societies. Sometimes, the work is simply delegated to individual committee members, but occasionally, as in the organization of many large arts festivals, a paid employee is hired to undertake the bulk of the work, reporting to the committee as and when necessary, once the committee has established the policy and approved the budget.

Quite often, the body which forms the 'standing' or 'ad hoc' committee will be a Registered Charity, in which case it must act in conformity with its charitable status.

Whatever mechanism is chosen to promote the programme or event, care must be taken in respect of the following:

- Choosing the correct 'vehicle' – an over-large committee may well cause problems.
- Identifying roles and responsibilities – this should be done on the basis of expertise and experience.
- Establishing the duties and powers of any paid employees, e.g. through a job description.
- Understanding the overall process – the need for forward planning, the importance of the feasibility study process, whether conducted formally or not.

The 'vehicle' or mechanism having been established, the planning process can begin in earnest. If a committee is used then its members will need to meet regularly, and any agendas/minutes prepared carefully by the Hon. Secretary, or perhaps by the Event Coordinator (howsoever titled) working through the Hon. Secretary.

Precise roles can be determined by the committee, with an agenda which requires that 'progress reports' be submitted on specific aspects, or upon the project as a whole.

Stage 5: Organization

The organization stage is most important, since all the commitments are made during this time. If the event or programme is being handled by a committee, then the members will need to meet on several occasions in order to reach agreement on what is to be promoted, i.e. the content and the form.

Similarly, if the event or programme is being promoted by an individual, then he or she must decide upon its precise nature. It is this stage which should see the following:

1   Decisions as to what is being promoted (Is it likely to be popular? How much will it cost?)
2   Decisions as to the appropriate venue (Is it available? Is it sufficiently large to accommodate the event and yield the necessary return? Does it have all the ancillary facilities?)
3   Decisions as to draft budget (Could the event/programme break even, or make a profit? What happens if it makes a loss?)
4   Decisions as to resources required, in order that commitments may be made, e.g. for hiring transport, goods, security, etc. (What is needed? When? How much will it cost?)
5   Decisions as to sponsorship arrangements (Who seeks sponsorship? What is on offer to the sponsors? Is 'sole' or 'joint' sponsorship being sought?)

As can be seen, this is the stage at which decisions are made in the light of a draft budget which shows that the event or programme is financially viable.

Chapter 7 demonstrates how a budget is built up, and precisely the same principles apply here. Care should be taken, however, to include all expenditure, and to avoid over-optimism on the matter of the income.

Stage 6: 'Refining'

The broad planning having been largely completed, the time has come to refine everything and to check all the details so that the programme or event will run smoothly. Contracts for hiring equipment, and any 'concessions' (also contracts, but sometimes based on percentage of turnover rather than site hire fees) should be double-checked by the Event Coordinator, making sure that the goods and the people will indeed 'turn up' at the right place at the correct time.

Outdoor events such as Town Shows are especially complicated, and the 'refining phase' is one which is extremely time-consuming but very important. Given the nature of such events, any item which has a bearing on safety and security – ensuring police/ambulance/fire services presence, installation of ground-wide Public Address System, erection of security fencing, delivery of short-wave radios (for stewards) and so on – is vital if the public is to receive the service which it can reasonably expect.

A highly systematic approach, and a clear sequence-duration planning model, is recommended for large outdoor events, for the simple reason that many of the particular items needed are not found 'on-site', as they would be with indoor venues, and their hire requires plenty of notice. Specialist caterers require at least a year's notice for summer events, for example, because they will already have regular commitments around the country. Similarly, marquees, spectator seating, and mobile toilets should be booked well in advance, as must any major acts, such as military bands. The 'refining' phase requires that all of the key written arrangements (contracts, exchange of letters, booking forms) are personally verified, e.g. by telephone or fax. Relying entirely on written communications conducted perhaps a year earlier is simply too risky.

Stage 7: 'Acquainting'

'Acquainting' means telling people about the programme or event, and represents the liaison/advisory function (e.g. with statutory authorities) as well as the marketing/publicity function. This phase will probably overlap with that which precedes it, depending on the nature of the promotion and the time scale associated with it.

Space does not allow for a detailed discussion of the marketing role, and there are in any case specialist texts on the subject. None the less, some points are worth making so that the reader may have some general guidelines to follow:

1   Marketing should be regarded as a key discipline, and appropriate expertise should be sought to handle the whole programme or event.
2   Marketing in general and publicity in particular should be planned carefully in advance, allowing lead-in times for the design process, artwork preparation, and printing where appropriate.

3   Publicity should make full use of the available United Kingdom spectrum as follows:

public sector radio (e.g. BBC), national and/or local
commercial radio (national and/or local)
public sector television (national/regional)
commercial television (terrestrial/satellite)
national press
local press
local 'free' newspaper (paid for through advertising)
large posters on billboard sites (managed commercially)
specialist magazines, of which there are now many
posters at strategic sites, including shop windows and public notice-boards
leaflets, distributed at key locations, depending on nature of programme or event, or delivered by local newsagents (at a small cost) at the same time as newspapers
programmes/brochures, also at key locations, such as shopping centres, libraries, entertainment/sport venues
street banners, at high street locations (check with local authority on whether planning consent is required)
display signs, usually at major 'road-entry' points into the town or city
computer-based data banks, providing 'event diary' information where these are available to the public, e.g. at libraries and tourist information centres
other printed 'listing' services, e.g. events 'diaries' in publications such as 'What's On' or 'Time Out' published by local authorities, plus lists of events published by some national voluntary bodies
verbal announcements, made on appropriate occasions, e.g. announcing the date of next year's arts festival at the end of this year's
electronic 'public information' panels, where available (found a great deal in France, but less so in the United Kingdom)
special displays or preliminary 'special events', providing many 'photo-opportunities'
word-of-mouth, where one potential customer tells another that the event is to take place
Internet services, where available.

Clearly not all of the above-mentioned opportunities or services are available to everyone, and a purely local promotion is unlikely to receive national publicity. Often, indeed, such promotions save a great deal of time and money by making use of the formal and informal 'networks' which already exist, e.g. by arranging for schools to send leaflets to pupils' parents, by circulating a notice to members of clubs and societies with compatible interests, and so on.

Whatever the scale of the publicity exercise, an appropriate budget for expenditure must be included within the draft budget. Detailed costing may be then be assembled, using quotations (from printers), newspaper 'rate cards' (showing cost-per-centimetre-column), plus any other materials or services required, such as designing a logo and preparing art work.

Stage 8: 'Turn out'

Turn out has two meanings in this context, the one being the 'final result' of the promotion, in terms of the numbers of people who do 'turn out' on the day or evening, and the second delineating the manager's responsibility for the promotion's overall appearance.

In either sense, the management has an important role, by ensuring that everything runs according to plan or, if contingency action has to be implemented, e.g. by substitutions, that customers still receive good value for money. Again, outdoor events demonstrate how important is contingency planning, especially for inclement weather conditions, but even the most straightforward show, whether amateur or professional, may be affected by laryngitis striking the main protagonist just before 'opening night'.

Promoters are expected to do the following:

- Make last-minute check of venue, particularly if hired from a third party, to ensure dressing rooms/changing rooms/toilets/auditorium/ancillary facilities are all clean and tidy.
- If venue is outdoor, check weather forecasts, and plan accordingly, e.g. car parking within fields is acceptable if the ground is dry, but not if conditions become very wet.
- Keep all copies of hiring documents, contracts with artistes, agreements with 'concessionaires' to hand, in case disputes arise without warning and need to be resolved quickly.
- Ensure that all internal communication systems are in working order before the event begins – this is particularly important with large outdoor events, at rugby/football stadia and such like.
- Ensure that all staff are appropriately dressed (stewards must be instantly recognizable, for example) and in their correct locations. Stewards must be fully briefed as to emergency procedures well beforehand.

- Ensure that, where appropriate, emergency services have unhindered access onto the site or within the complex, and that any relevant systems, such as CCTV monitors, are in working order.
- Check that everything is in place immediately before the first customer arrives, simply by walking around the site or venue, looking at the place as if this were a first visit. Hospitality arrangements for VIPs and sponsors should also be checked personally, as should artistes' dressing rooms and changing areas.
- Immediately after the event, thanks should be communicated to:
  (a) The customers/audience/spectators – personally or through P.A. systems (a personal 'thank you for coming' as customers left the building used to be the hallmark of a good cinema manager, some years ago)
  (b) The staff of the venue – personally where possible
  (c) The sponsors – personally on the day(s), and reiterate afterwards by letter
  (d) The emergency services (police, ambulance, fire) – personally if possible, but if not then by letter to respective head of operational unit.

Stage 9: Evaluation

This is the final phase of the cycle, and if the promotion is to be repeated, will form the feedback which essentially guides the first three phases of that second programme or event.

Evaluation takes place immediately after the promotion and, provided that they have been correctly devised, will use the performance indicators referred to earlier. A set of final accounts may also be prepared – and where appropriate agreed by a committee – showing the 'actual' income and expenditure, and therefore net loss or net profit, as against those which were projected or estimated.

Learning from the past

Where the promotion is to be repeated, the evaluation needs to be formalized and recorded. The first committee meeting or individual consideration of the 'repeat cycle' should therefore assess the feedback information at the outset of the next staged exercise, and should decide upon the following:

- Was the promotion a success or not, having regard to its objectives, and to its performance indicators?

- Was the venue itself adequate? Should it be used again or should an alternative (smaller or larger) one be sought?
- Did everything go smoothly, i.e. was the 'form' appropriate, and was the 'content' of the right quality?
- Were all the resources adequate for the purpose? Did they represent good value for money?
- Did the planning/refining process operate correctly? Are more/less committee meetings needed, for example?
- Was the liaison function carried out properly, and were the emergency services satisfied with the way that the event had been handled. In this respect, some feedback from those services would also be useful.

Three points remain to be mentioned before we leave the subject of feedback:

1 Promoters need to ask themselves whether the promotion should be repeated in the same form, even if the last one was so successful. Some variety (of 'content' certainly) is essential to maintain public interest, and a new component (e.g. adding lasers to firework displays) helps to make the publicity that much easier to achieve.
2 Promoters need to check if any new rules or regulations have appeared subsequent to the last promotion which might conceivably affect the next one. This is particularly important with outdoor events and with catering services. Advice can normally be obtained on this issue from the insurance company which provided the necessary 'cover', and from the local authority.
3 Promoters should examine the actual process of organization, whichever method was adopted, and decide if changes need to be made, e.g. earlier liaison with licensing authorities, greater involvement with local clubs and societies, etc.

Legislative framework

Finally, attention must be paid to the legislative framework which surrounds and relates to the promotion. Many aspects of this framework are described in Chapter 2 , but some specific points would be appropriate here.

Health and safety/duty of care

Both spectators and artistes/participants must be protected from harm, as far as possible, in accordance with:

1   specific legislation e.g. Fire Safety and Safety in Places of Sport Act 1987
2   general legislation, e.g. Health and Safety at Work etc. Act 1974
3   general principles, as implicit in legal judgements regarding 'duty of care', or explicit in legislation relating to occupiers' liability.

Contracts

Programmes and events may involve one or more of the following:

1   Contracts with venues – for hire of venue, support staff, ancillary facilities
2   Contracts with ticket agencies – for sale of tickets at various points, a service normally paid for on a percentage basis
3   Contracts with marketing agencies – for publicity-production and distribution
4   Contracts with artistes – arranged either directly or through an agent
5   Contracts with suppliers (purchase or hire) – for supply of goods, e.g. mobile radios. P.A. systems, printed material, poster sites, etc.
6   Contracts with sponsors – often completed through an 'exchange of letters'
7   Contracts with 'concessionaires' – where sites are hired out as 'points of sale', either for a straight fee or a percentage.

Sale of goods

Any goods sold during the course of the promotion must conform to legislation which relates to:

1   advertising
2   product liability
3   suitability for purposes intended.

These requirements are explained in Chapter 2.

Liability for belongings

If a participant is 'invited' to make use of changing facilities, and a locker supplied within those changing rooms, then the participant may assume that any goods left in the room, or more probably in the locker, are being looked after by the management. Each venue may differ slightly in design and layout, but notices should be checked as to their words regarding 'liability' – though the point has previously been made that notices alone may not protect the management from a claim.

Similarly, a 'lost property service' must itself be secure, so that property is not stolen whilst 'under protection', or falsely claimed.

Protection and control of spectators

The control of spectators is a corollary of safety aspects referred to above. Obviously, the risks are greatest where the crowd is largest and where there is an element of conflict, as at certain football matches. In this connection, the Safety of Sports Grounds Act 1975 and the Fire Safety and Safety at Places of Sport Act 1987 may require that the stadium is licensed by the local authority, in conjunction with other statutory bodies (e.g. Fire Service and Police) and in accordance with any applicable codes or guidelines, such as the 'Green Book'.

Sale of food and drink

Where food and drink are being sold by concessionaires, it is wise to insert a clause within their respective contracts which obliges them to obtain the necessary licences, and to liaise (in the case of unwrapped food sales) with the local authority's environmental health department. Liquor sales, at venues other than licensed premises, are often handled by publicans, who hold an on-licence, or, in the case of large outdoor events, by specialist companies.

Insurance

Advice should be obtained from either an Insurance Broker or from the company which already provides insurance cover for the venue, where anything out of the ordinary is proposed. Insurance can be arranged for the following:

1 Public liability, i.e. accidents to third parties
2 Accidents to staff
3 Accidents caused by one participant upon another (sometimes termed 'member-to-member' cover)
4 Theft of goods or equipment, e.g. items that are borrowed or hired
5 Loss of income caused by bad weather (sometimes termed 'pluvial cover').

Regard must be paid to the Employers' Liability (Compulsory Insurance) Act 1969, which requires that employers provide insurance cover for their employees, against liability for 'bodily harm, injury and disease' sustained through the course of their employment.

Conclusions

Managing events and programmes is an exhilarating experience, and can be extremely fulfilling when a successful project is made available to an appreciative audience. Outdoor events can also be very successful, if everything runs to plan: the parachutes open, the lasers work properly, the band arrives and so on.

However, as existing managers will be aware, things can quickly go wrong: the 'star' may cancel, the weather prevents the parachuting, the lasers don't work, and the coach bringing the band breaks down ...

No book such as this can ever prevent such spanners from being thrown into such works. All it can do is to make the planning process a little smoother, by identifying where the spanners might come from.

References and recommended reading

A Practical Approach to the Administration of Leisure and Recreation Services. (1992). Croner Publications Ltd. (See Chapter 7, 'Organizing and Planning Events', which includes a useful checklist.)

Torkildsen, G. (1983). *Leisure and Recreation Management.* E. & F.N. Spon. (See also subsequent editions.)

Watt, D. (1998). *Event Management in Leisure and Tourism.* Longman.

7 Managing risk

Questions

At the end of this chapter you should be able to undertake the following:

1 Consider the degree to which leisure customers have unique characteristics, and the extent to which these characteristics accentuate the risks which they face.
2 Examine one major 'leisure accident', such as Summerland, Bradford or Hillsborough, and indicate the extent to which crowd psychology influenced the outcome.
3 Indicate how leisure organizations may reduce the hazards which could affect staff, customers and contractors within their domain.

Introduction

The particular characteristics of the 'leisure experience' are such that 'risk management' is becoming a major concern. Put simply, the variability of some leisure environments, when combined with the unpredictable behaviour of many customers, can lead to disaster.

Secondly, it must be recognized that the actual range of customers – from trained adults to vulnerable children – presents serious management problems, as does the mixture of individuals and groups within the same leisure environment.

Thirdly, we see that the presence of large numbers of people, especially at sporting events, creates a potential catastrophe, as at Bradford, Hillsborough, and Guatemala City.

In no other sphere is risk management so essential but so problematical. In no other sphere is legislation becoming so onerous, licensing so substantial, insurance so important – and litigation so worrying.

This chapter endeavours to look at some of the issues involved, at some accident statistics, and at the principles of risk assessment and risk management. It also looks at accidents in specific parts of the leisure industry – where risk is arguably greatest – in the hope that some tentative conclusions may be reached about future developments.

Guidance as to 'best practice' is implicit within the text, and this may be of value in countries which have different legal frameworks to the United Kingdom.

Before moving from the aspect of 'special characteristics' which opened the chapter, some contrast with other industries might emphasize the point and thereby the particular responsibilities of the leisure manager.

Consider, for example, the construction industry, where accidents are common. Here we see a combination of the following: variable weather and ground conditions/moving equipment/heavy machinery/vehicles/people working at heights. All such conditions create a substantial risk. Accident rates for the building industry have always been greater than for other industries, but imagine how much higher they would be if parties of youngsters were brought to play on the sites, or if retired folk could wander around the place unsupervised.

Then consider a theme park – with variable weather and ground conditions, 'white-knuckle' rides soaring to considerable heights, and other mechanical features such as merry-go-rounds. Perhaps the point is clear: leisure environments can be every bit as dangerous as other environments, and the risks are accentuated by the behavioural characteristics of the human beings on the site.

Mortality statistics

Mortality statistics make the same stark point, and demonstrate that while the leisure industry is about 'fun', it can also be deadly serious. Figure 7.1 shows work-related mortality rates for the United Kingdom, from 1981 to 1994/95. Work-related deaths include those which occur in various facilities, whether leisure-based or not, but do not include deaths which occur in unmanaged environments, such as mountaineering fatalities. Had the fatality occurred during the course of an organized programme, however, it would be incorporated into the figures.

The graph shows two massive increases in mortality rates. The first increase represents the Bradford fire disaster, when 56 people died as a result of a fire catching hold in one of the stands, the second increase represents Hillsborough, when 96 fans died as a result of the crush which followed a 'crowd surge' onto the site just before the match was to begin.

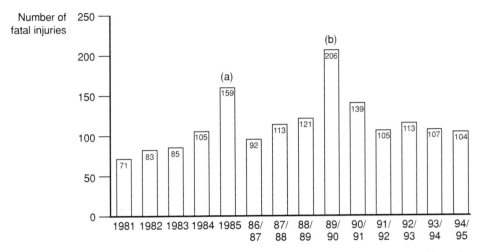

Figure 7.1   Fatal injuries to members of the UK public, in an organizational/work context, 1981–1994/5. *Source*: Health and Safety Executive. (Data includes (a) 56 fatalities in the Bradford City Football Club disaster and (b) 96 fatalities in the Hillsborough Stadium disaster)

These tragedies apart, the number and nature of accidents within the leisure environment – whether or not the environment is 'managed' – are such that they must be taken seriously. As fewer people work in heavy industries, the building trade or farming, it may be that leisure-related accidents will become more significant, comparatively speaking. Certainly the litigation which follows leisure-related accidents is growing more substantial, and so is the anxiety of insurance companies who keep a watchful eye on the number of cases and the scale of settlements.

Accident statistics

The Royal Society for the Prevention of Accidents (RoSPA) carried out an interesting exercise some years ago (1990) when it examined information gathered by the Consumer Safety Unit of the Department of Trade and Industry.

The Unit collected its information from 11 casualty departments within major hospitals across the United Kingdom, and gave some idea of the scale, cause and consequence of sports-related accidents, from which some extrapolation might be made.

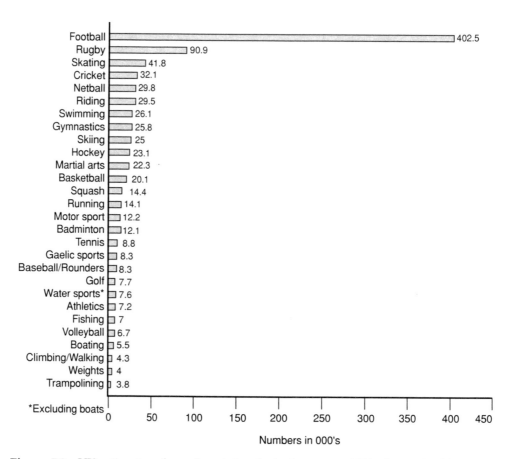

Figure 7.2   UK estimates of numbers injured playing sport, 1989. *Source*: LASS, DTI (1995)

The General Household Survey of 1987 was also used to provide some information on sports participation, although the questions in the survey and scale of responses were not such that conclusive statements could be made about degrees of risk attached to specific sports.

None the less, the information is fascinating. Figure 7.2 shows, for example, that football is the 'injury leader', with an estimated 402 500 hospitalized cases, followed by rugby with an estimated 90 900 hospitalized cases. Not surprisingly perhaps, ice-skating injuries come next (41 800 cases), followed by cricket injuries (32 100 cases).

The appearance of trampolining at the bottom of the list may also seem surprising, given the risks involved. However, information on accident numbers alone

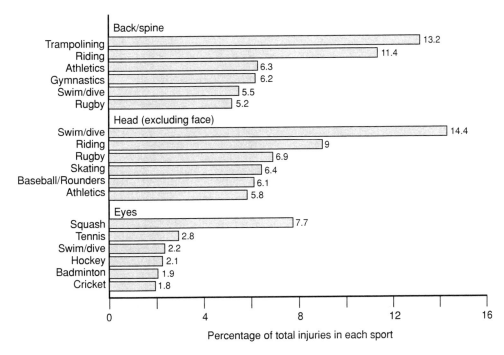

Figure 7.3 Sports leading to the most back, head and eye injuries. *Source*: LASS, DTI (1995)

may not show a full picture, particularly in relation to activities like trampolining and horse-riding, where serious injuries can occur. Trampolining leads the back/spinal injury 'league' at 13.2 per cent, whereas riding appears prominently in both back/spine and head injury tables. Figure 7.3 graphically provides the relevant information.

Accident statistics – fatalities

Mercifully, except for deaths which relate to the above-mentioned stadia disasters, the number of leisure-related fatalities is relatively modest. The Society of Public Health (1990) examined data assembled for England and Wales by the Office of Population Censuses and Surveys between 1982 and 1988. The study suggested that excluding drownings, the greatest number of deaths was due to horse-riding, followed by air-sports, motor sport, mountaineering and climbing. When the figures were modified to take account of 'exposure time', the study concluded that the mountaineering and motor sports were the most hazardous pursuits, followed by horse-riding. By way of comparison, the study surmised that mountaineering was at least 100 times and motor sports 50 times more hazardous than either ball games or watersports.

Accident statistics – drownings

RoSPA reported that 1996 had seen the second lowest recorded total for accidental drownings in 14 years, with a total of 441. Of these, drownings in rivers and streams made up 143, coastal drownings 122, drownings in lakes and reservoirs 69 and canal drownings 31. Drownings in swimming pools remained relatively low, at 10, and were significantly lower than the number of drownings in 'baths at home', at 38.

More will be said on the subject of drownings, later in the chapter.

DTI statistics

As has been mentioned earlier, the Department of Trade and Industry, through its Consumer Safety Unit, collects data on accidents in the United Kingdom. Its Annual Report for 1995 (the most recent available at the time of writing) points out that some 14 million people are treated at Accident and Emergency Units each year, and that 20 per cent of these are due to 'home accidents'. The number of 'home fatalities' (4000) also demands that attention be paid to this aspect of risk.

To an extent, the DTI Report is concerned with 'product liability', since the emphasis of its information is upon consumer products rather than on behaviour patterns. The Home Accident Surveillance System (HASS) collects data from 18 major hospitals, as does the Leisure Accident Surveillance System (LASS).

The report goes on to mention that data from 11 of the hospitals has been passed to the Commission of the European Community for inclusion in the European Home and Leisure Accident Surveillance System (EHLASS).

Accident locations are also quite revealing and rather curious. For example, it appears that four people aged over 75 were injured at public playgrounds. Other statistics are easier to explain, perhaps, where leisure facilities are involved. Table 7.1 provides information extracted from DTI statistics on 'location of accidents by age', by selecting those which might conceivably have a 'leisure connection'.

The scale of the problem becomes more startling if one looks at the last column, where, on the basis of extrapolation, the figures are projected to a national scale.

Table 7.1 Location of accidents, by age

Location			Age in years				National estimates (000s)
	0–4	5–14	15–64	65–74	75+	Un-known	
Hotel, B&B, YEA	8	15	117	12	10	0	6
Inside creche/nursery	163	15	7	0	0	0	7
School playground	264	2860	208	2	2	3	122
Education – indoor sport facility	11	1129	543	0	0	1	62
Education – swimming pool	1	31	8	0	0	0	0 (i.e. less than 1000)
Indoor sport facility	22	601	1590	10	3	5	82
Outdoor sport area	13	1004	5361	18	9	14	235
Swimming pool – indoor	35	201	128	8	3	2	14
Swimming pool – outdoor	3	16	25	2	0	0	2
Swimming pool – unspecified	18	118	96	3	0	1	9
Stables	5	68	101	2	0	0	6
Golf course	0	11	80	6	4	0	4
Unspecified sport area	6	227	944	3	0	1	43
Fairground/circus/zoo	23	95	130	1	5	0	9
Dance hall/disco	4	22	216	1	1	1	9
Bar/pub/social club	60	87	572	26	24	4	28
Restaurant/café	36	17	67	9	12	1	5
Cinema/theatre	2	9	30	5	4	0	2
Public playground	188	622	98	2	3	1	33
Social centre	28	153	130	11	22	2	13
Other leisure facility	56	356	494	20	20	1	35
Camp/caravan site	12	55	61	9	2	0	5
Parkland/cemetery	202	929	767	37	29	3	72
Country/pasture/wood	45	575	890	68	21	0	58
Waterside beach	29	143	307	22	7	2	19
In water	5	121	316	11	4	1	17
On board a vessel	1	10	47	7	0	0	2
Other natural area	5	31	131	6	0	0	6

Source: LASS, DTI (1995).

Thus, for example, outdoor sports areas saw approximately 235 000 accidents, school playgrounds 122 000, indoor sports facilities 82 000, parkland/cemeteries 72 000, education sector indoor sports facilities 62 000, and country/pasture/woods 58 000.

Though the figures are remarkable, they cannot explain all of the idiosyncrasies. Some of the categories of 'location' are slightly odd (e.g. parkland/cemeteries), while the age-banding chosen in the third column (15–64) is really too wide.

It should be noted, incidentally, that the DTI tables exclude 'accidents which occur in the course of paid employment', since such information is reported differently, and one hopes comprehensively, through procedures established through RIDDOR.

Three other tables from the 1995 DTI report are also considered to be relevant. Table 7.2 shows the activity of the patient at the time of the accident; Table 7.3 shows the sporting activity within which the accident occurred, by age and sex; and Table 7.4 shows the type of injuries which relate to specific sporting activities.

Football injuries appear to predominate in 'total percentage terms', as has been mentioned previously. In most of the sports listed, injuries sustained by males (of whatever age) tend to exceed injuries suffered by females – which itself reflects gender differences within sports participation. If we examine the 5–14 and 15–64 age groups, we see that the only exceptions to this are: gymnastics (both age groups), animal sport (both age groups, and probably horse-riding), winter sport (younger group only) and exercise/fitness (younger group only, probably gymnastics). The same table shows how certain sports are associated with a large number of accidents at certain ages e.g. football – and how few people receive sports injuries once they are over 65. However, the statistics for males aged 15–64 in 'stick/sport' is a little odd, and may reflect a greater degree of male participation in hockey.

Consequences of accidents

Since this chapter is concerned with 'accidents to human beings', it follows that accidents which are purely 'environmental', e.g. those caused by serious pollution, are not examined, though of course the effect of such accidents upon flora and fauna can be massive. 'Accidents', in our context, happen only to people (customers, staff, contractors, subcontractors), since it is generally people who sue, and not endangered species.

Civil action

Quite apart from the physical pain brought out by the accident, other consequences must be considered. Subsequent physical pain and suffering is taken into

Table 7.2 Activity of patient at time of the accident.

Activity category	Age in years					Unknown	Row totals	%	National estimate (000s)
	0–4	5–14	15–64	65–74	75+				
Household activity	3	11	69	1	6	0	90	0.1	3
DIY/maintenance	0	19	379	9	3	0	410	0.5	15
Shopping	80	39	462	234	250	3	1068	1.3	39
Education/training	32	2991	1046	1	0	2	4072	5.1	149
Sport (excl. education)	73	5136	14679	57	21	41	20007	24.9	731
Play/hobby/leisure	1480	6962	2243	82	48	15	10830	13.5	396
Basic needs	464	1363	3069	450	597	22	5965	7.4	218
Travelling/touring	417	2463	4952	651	653	13	9149	11.4	334
Other/unspecified activity	1806	8968	15309	1257	1373	123	28836	35.9	1054
Column totals	4355	27952	42208	2742	2951	219	80427	100	2940
%	5.4	34.8	52.5	3.4	3.7	0.3	100	–	–
National estimate (000s)	159	1022	1543	100	108	8	2940	–	–

Source: LASS, DTI (1995).

Table 7.3 Sporting activity at time of accident by age and sex.

Sports category	0–4 Sex		5–14 Sex			15–64 Sex			65–74 Sex		75+ Sex		Unknown Sex		Row totals	%	National estimate (000s)
	M	F	M	F	U	M	F	U	M	F	M	F	M	F			
Athletics	0	0	26	18	0	144	45	0	2	0	1	0	0	0	236	1.2	9
Gymnastics	3	2	23	90	0	8	41	0	0	0	0	0	0	1	168	0.8	6
Stick/etc., sport	4	2	222	131	0	1382	453	1	18	9	5	1	1	1	2230	11.1	82
Ball sport – no stick	18	4	2916	382	1	9074	645	1	5	6	6	4	24	2	13088	65.4	478
Combat sport	0	1	114	35	0	442	94	0	0	0	0	0	2	0	688	3.4	25
Shooting	0	0	4	1	0	17	6	0	0	1	1	0	0	0	30	0.1	1
Wheel sport	2	2	161	136	0	374	67	0	0	0	0	0	2	0	744	3.7	27
Animal sport	1	2	15	120	0	51	241	0	0	1	0	0	0	1	432	2.2	16
Winter sport	2	3	154	161	0	287	252	0	0	1	0	0	1	0	861	4.3	31
Landscape sport	2	0	6	1	0	34	15	0	0	0	0	1	1	0	60	0.3	2
Water sport	16	8	180	114	0	318	123	0	7	2	2	0	1	0	771	3.9	28
Air sport	0	0	0	0	0	32	11	0	0	0	0	0	0	0	43	0.2	2
Exercise/fitness	1	0	10	19	0	119	95	0	1	3	0	0	1	0	249	1.2	9
Other/unspecified sport	0	0	61	35	0	255	50	2	1	0	0	0	3	0	407	2.0	15
Totals	49	24	3892	1243	1	12537	2138	4	34	23	15	6	36	5	20007	100	731

Source: LASS, DTI (1995).

Table 7.4 Sporting activity by type of injury.

Sport category	Super-ficial injury	Open wound	Burn	Bruise/ contusion	Con-cussion	Other soft tissue injury	Bone injury	Joint tendon injury	Chem-ical injury	Sys-temic injury	Non-injurous FB	No diagnosed injury	Other injury	Un-specified injury	Row totals	%	National estimate (000s)
Athletics	14	24	2	20	2	116	28	76	3	0	0	8	9	3	305	1.2	11
Gymnastics	1	2	0	26	0	102	27	39	0	0	0	5	6	2	210	0.8	8
Stick/etc. sport	50	352	1	433	38	1066	349	410	5	0	3	26	99	43	2875	11.5	105
Ball sport – no stick	304	1151	0	2122	237	6314	2424	2555	14	0	10	246	377	266	16020	63.9	586
Combat sport	5	38	0	125	14	372	122	106	0	0	0	11	17	24	834	3.3	30
Shooting	4	16	0	5	0	7	3	2	0	0	0	0	3	0	40	0.2	1
Wheel sport	92	74	5	131	21	349	236	92	2	0	1	16	28	11	1058	4.2	39
Animal sport	41	26	0	111	33	284	95	65	0	0	1	12	17	13	698	2.8	26
Winter sport	23	73	3	172	7	427	228	134	0	0	0	7	31	14	1119	4.5	41
Landscape sport	7	10	0	10	0	27	13	12	0	0	3	0	2	1	85	0.3	3
Water sport	66	225	9	131	27	262	58	69	11	4	8	26	60	13	969	3.9	35
Air sport	3	5	0	2	1	20	17	3	0	0	0	1	1	3	56	0.2	2
Exercise/fitness	5	21	0	38	3	114	28	85	0	0	1	3	8	4	310	1.2	11
Other/unspecified sport	18	38	0	62	6	169	57	92	1	1	0	11	26	27	508	2.0	19
Totals	633	2055	20	3388	389	9629	3685	3740	36	5	27	372	684	424	25087	100	917

Source: LASS, DTI (1995).

account by the courts, in calculating any damages which are ultimately awarded, as well as 'psychological suffering' or stress brought about by the accident. 'Loss of earnings', however, is frequently the largest figure of all. The solicitor acting on behalf of the injured person will make use of medical evidence, in identifying physical and psychological consequences of the accident. Assessors, who are well versed in such matters, can calculate the financial costs. And so the claim escalates, since it may comprise the following:

- calculations with regard to initial physical pain and suffering
- calculations as to future physical pain and suffering
- initial and subsequent psychological harm
- loss of earnings related to periods of treatment, and convalescence/recuperation
- costs of solicitors plus assessors/medical evidence/counsel's advice
- cost of medical treatment
- cost of special equipment/home care, etc. consequent upon the accident.

In such circumstances, it is hardly surprising that so many cases are settled 'out of court', as defendants (i.e. those being sued in the civil action) realize the stakes involved.

Criminal prosecution

Where an act or omission is regarded by the state as being of a 'criminal nature', then it is pursued by the Crown Prosecution Service (CPS) and not by an aggrieved individual. It is of course open to individuals to take a 'private action' through the civil courts quite separately.

Accidents which occur as a result of negligence may be so serious as to merit a criminal prosecution, as with the Lyme Bay case, when the charge of criminal negligence was effectively upheld as a consequence of serious breaches of the Health and Safety at Work etc. Act 1974. In effect, the company involved made English legal history by becoming the first company to be convicted of homicide; its managing director, likewise, became the first director to receive an immediate custodial sentence (three years, reduced on appeal to two) for a manslaughter conviction arising from the operation of a business. His company was additionally fined £60 000 (this case is examined later in the chapter).

The potential for criminal prosecution should never be under-estimated, particularly where, in the United Kingdom at least, so many wrongs or torts are now regarded as 'criminal', whereas previously they may have been seen as 'civil matters' or merely 'acts of fate' (or God). Food hygiene is one example, where more and more legislation has appeared, where licensing authorities have been given greater powers, and where criminal prosecutions (as well as civil actions) have been pursued after deaths caused by food contamination.

Other consequences of accidents

These may be described as relating to reputation, time and finance though all three are connected, e.g. loss of reputation could have a serious financial impact.

Loss of reputation

Publicity will inevitably affect reputation, when initial coverage of a death, or major injury is supplemented by coverage of the court case, in the press and possibly on television, where the matter is considered to be 'criminal'. Generally speaking, civil actions receive far less publicity, unless the final settlement establishes a new precedent, or breaks the record for damages.

Reputations take many years to recover, since public confidence will be shaken by the publicity. Some firms never recover from the media attention, and simply 'go under'. The opprobrium attached to them may become associated with the sector as a whole, as it was for a while with outdoor activity centres after the Lyme Bay tragedy.

Loss of time

Considerable time has also to be expended to defend a case, whether it is being pursued in the civil or criminal courts. Time means money in the sense that staff who might otherwise have been deployed elsewhere (to run the business and generate income) have to prepare statements, assemble evidence, spend time with solicitors, and so on – quite apart from the time which may be taken up by formal briefings, interviews with solicitors or barristers, and travel, court protocol and the court case itself.

Financial cost

Financial expenditure – on 'time taken up', loss of revenue through effect upon reputation, and on hiring expert legal (and perhaps medical) opinion – is likely to be very substantial indeed. Loss of income, caused by a loss of custom, can lead to bankruptcy.

It should be evident from what has been said that accidents are best avoided, and that efforts made to do so are likely to be much more effective than efforts made to contest a claim once it has been received. The legal principle which enjoins managers to exercise the 'common duty of care' (see Chapter 2) should not in any case replace the simple ethical idea of 'doing unto others as you would wish to be done by'.

Ethical codes, though, are implicit, and are not really adequate for today's purposes, where 'criminalization', 'codification' and a mass of legislation are making so many imperatives explicit. Once made explicit, the words enter the public domain, in the form of acts of parliament, regulations, codes of practice and so forth. They cannot then be ignored, certainly not by managers who, the law assumes, should know the words and their implications.

As rules have become more explicit, so other rules have been formulated to ensure 'procedures' and not just 'outcomes'. Risk assessment procedures are one such example, where the procedure itself becomes a rule or legal necessity – at which point risk assessment becomes a compulsory process and not just 'best practice'. As we shall see later, that is now the case. But before we do so, some 'models of risk' need to be examined.

Models of risk

In essence, the risk of accidents occurs when the behaviour of the customer meets with the physical characteristics of the leisure environment, though there are occasions when the behaviour of one 'leisure customer' jeopardizes the well-being of another, e.g. in cases of competitive team sports, or at crowded leisure venues.

The leisure manager can have no legal responsibility for the customer's behaviour whilst that customer is off-site; likewise, excepting a legal duty to trespassers and passers-by, the leisure manager need have no anxieties about accidents if there are no customers, staff or contractors present within the facility or site.

A simple model such as Figure 7.4 shows what is meant: the left-hand circle represents the physical characteristics of the leisure environment, and the right circle the behavioural characteristics of the customer. The overlap represents the theoretical area where accidents could occur.

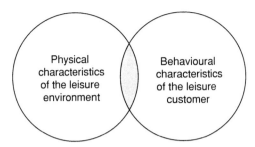

Figure 7.4 A theoretical model of risk where leisure environment interacts with leisure customer

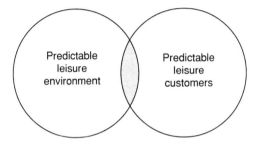

Figure 7.5 A predictable environment combines with predictable customers (Model 1)

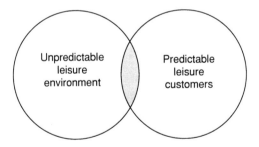

Figure 7.6 An unpredictable environment combines with predictable customers (Model 2)

Further elaboration explains more about the nature of the risk, by adding the notions of 'predictable' and 'unpredictable'. Thus we have four models, each of which represents a range of leisure facilities or programmes.

These simple models (Figures 7.5, 7.6, 7.7 and 7.8) demonstrate the difference between leisure managers and their counterparts in other industries. Retail

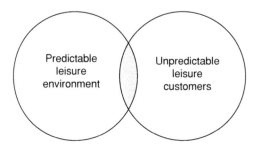

Figure 7.7   A predictable environment combines with unpredictable customers
(Model 3)

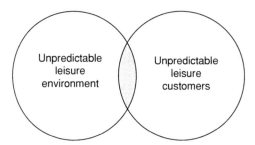

Figure 7.8   An unpredictable environment combines with unpredictable customers
(Model 4)

managers, for example, will be responsible for buildings which stay roughly the same, (predictable environment) where products are quality controlled, where lighting, temperature, and humidity are all predetermined. Supermarket customers generally behave in a straightforward manner (predictable behaviour) and do not seek out risks in order to make their visit more exciting. In such a context, the physical environment is almost completely predictable, and the behaviour of customers likewise.

Even on building sites – where the highest number of accidents at work occur – there may often be an unpredictable environment, but the behaviour of a trained work force is relatively predictable.

That leads to a further assumption, which is that training reduces the likelihood of random behaviour, and thereby increases predictability. Training does not, of course, create 'absolute predictability', and indeed no human being can ever be so. Naturally, there will be occasions when experienced hill-walkers fail to tell friends about their route, when trained athletes push their bodies too far, when qualified balloonists misjudge a landing and so forth. The point is that training creates a degree of predictability, because the rules are common. The trained person is more likely to behave in a predictable way than someone who is untrained simply through the process of 'internalization', whereby the same rules are observed equally by everyone.

By matching the four models to different leisure facilities, we can perhaps see where operational problems may occur and where risks may escalate beyond control.

Model 1:   Predictable environment/predictable customers, e.g. concert hall, art gallery/museum visit, bowling green competition

Model 2:   Unpredictable environment/predictable customers, e.g. yachting competition, white-water canoeing event, professional mountaineering expedition, orienteering event

Model 3:   Predictable environment/unpredictable customers, e.g. public swimming pool, theme park, water park visits

Model 4:   Unpredictable environment/unpredictable customers, e.g. outdoor activity centre, jet-ski hire centre, hill walking or canoeing (by untrained individuals), horse-riding, pony trekking (also by untrained individuals).

The risks increase through models 1 to 4, and therefore the manager's role is slightly different for each one.

A 'model 1 manager' is fortunate in that the leisure environment is relatively stable, and does not change from day to day, or from moment to moment. The 'quality of experience' can be assured, and perhaps innovation introduced in such a way as to create a more varied environment – as at the various museums where interactive displays fulfil precisely that role.

A 'model 2 manager' expects to have customers who are trained and experienced, and predominantly adults. Care needs to be taken to ensure that the customers are, indeed, qualified and/or experienced, and that they understand the implication of an unpredictable environment. This is particularly true of maritime activities, where sea and estuary conditions may change rapidly due to tidal currents and wind speeds.

A 'model 3 manager' is probably the most common, and is often concerned with problems caused by customer behaviour, whether that behaviour is unpredictable by nature or downright malicious by intent. Frequently, the risks attached to the use of the leisure environment are derived from customer behaviour, and not from the qualities of the environment itself.

A 'model 4 manager' has the hardest task of all, in terms of risk assessment and risk management, since both environment and customer are unpredictable. Risk assessment becomes a crucial exercise, as do customer monitoring and customer control.

Crowd behaviour: A variation to the model

Some activities and facilities do not fit well into these structures, especially where the 'customers' actually 'become' the environment in some measure. Major tragedies can occur at stadia when the crowd itself begins to move, for whatever cause. Often that initial cause has nothing to do with the physical condition of the venue, but everything to do with the psychology of the crowd itself. Once the crowd begins to move, however, the design of the venue has its effect.

Accidents at stadia

At the Hillsborough Stadium in Sheffield, 96 fans died on 15 April 1989, when the ground became over-crowded, and the crowd pushed people downwards against the fencing which at that time protected the pitch from 'fan invasions'.

Guatemala City on 17 October 1996 was the scene of a similar tragedy, when 83 people died and 180 were injured prior to the kick-off at a World Cup match. The stadium had seating for 45 000, but it later appeared that many more fans, some bearing forged tickets, forced their way through the entrance gates. Football's international governing body, FIFA, concluded that the panic began when fans left outside kicked down an entrance door in the south stand, pushing other spectators downwards to the seats below.

These two disasters, Hillsborough and Guatemala City were similar, not only in their magnitude but in their cause: the over-crowding before the match even began, a crush in a particular zone, and fans trapped against the fencing around the pitch. Indeed, the connection was noted in the *Daily Telegraph* of 18 October 1989, when it quoted the words of the chairman of the Hillsborough Family Support Group, who on hearing the Guatemala incident said that in a matter of five minutes, he relived Hillsborough all over again. 'It came flooding back, and I felt physically sick', he is reported to have said; 'the lessons of Hillsborough haven't been learned'.

In accidents such as this, the crowd or the 'aggregated customers', become a very special kind of environment. It was therefore 'people' and not 'structures' who were initially the cause of the disaster of Hillsborough and at Guatemala.

Serious accidents have occurred at stadia elsewhere, notably Mexico City (1985), Port-au-Prince, Haiti (1976), Buenos Aires (1968) and Lima (1964).

Summerland

The situation at Summerland was slightly different, but once again demonstrates how leisure can be a deadly serious business. In 1973, some 50 people died, and a similar number were injured, when a relatively new leisure complex on the Isle of Man caught fire.

The official enquiry (Summerland Fire Commission, 1974) into the tragedy makes grim but fascinating reading, since in this particular instance the 'crowd responses' were less to blame for the deaths than were the deficiencies in the design and management of the leisure complex. The tragedy shocked the United Kingdom, and was one of the earliest 'leisure accidents' in the country for many years.

One particular passage (Conclusions, para. 241) is especially pertinent, sending as it does a vital message to future generations of 'leisure architects' and leisure managers:

> Architects in designing buildings must not rely upon efficient management to make the building efficient and safe in time of emergency or failure, but neither must the occupiers accept the building as safe without knowing something of its vulnerability of fabric and contents and without a considerable study of the problems that arise due to the usage and occupancy of the kind of clientele which they are encouraging.

The manager's role

If we use the models as described earlier, with the caveat that some leisure experiences do not fit into any of the models (e.g. a crowd becomes more significant than the built environment), then we can say something about the manager's role in relation to 'risk identification'. Thus managers should:

- understand the nature of the physical environment for which he or she is responsible
- appreciate the risks which the physical environment may contain once the customer's behaviour enters into the frame.

Risk assessment

United Kingdom legislation

Risk assessment is itself a simple notion. Leisure managers in the past knew intuitively what the risks were, and acted (again intuitively) to reduce these risks.

There was no formula for risk assessment nor any legal requirement to carry out such a procedure.

Since the 1970s, the position in the United Kingdom has changed considerably. Two Acts of Parliament have given rise to regulations which make risk assessment compulsory. One of the Acts was designed primarily for the workplace but applies equally to the leisure industry as elsewhere; the other arose directly from the canoeing tragedy which occurred at Lyme Bay in March 1993. They are:

- The Health and Safety at Work etc. Act 1974
- The Activity Centres (Young Persons' Safety) Act 1995.

Each of the two Acts contains clauses which allow subsequent regulations to be made 'by order' of the respective Minister. Such regulations are tacitly approved by Parliament, having been 'laid' before that body for a standard period. Incidentally, regulations made in this way are not to be confused with European Union Regulations, which are made in a completely different manner. EU regulations apply throughout the whole of the Union, whereas the regulations referred to below are applicable purely to the United Kingdom.

Those regulations which require employers to carry out risk assessment procedures are as follows.

Under the 1974 Act:
Control of Substances Hazardous to Health Regulations 1988 (COSHH)
Noise at Work Regulations 1989
Management of Health and Safety at Work Regulations 1992
Personal Protective Equipment at Work Regulations 1992
Manual Handling Operations Regulations 1992
Health and Safety (Display Screen Equipment) Regulations 1992

Under the 1995 Act:
The Adventure Activities Licensing Regulations 1996

Clearly, 1992 was a good year for the implementation of regulations, many of which could not have been foreseen when the 1974 Act was devised – fewer workers spent their time in front of VDU screens, for example, and therefore no regulations were needed.

The Adventure Activities Licensing Regulations are a different matter altogether, since both they and the 1995 Act from which they sprang are a direct result of a single accident. And since these regulations apply uniquely to one sector of the leisure industry, it is fascinating to see what risk assessment procedures are set out. The general information provided to applicants by the licensing body, the Adventure Activities Licensing Authority, states that:

> to obtain a licence you will be required to demonstrate to the licensing authority that you follow good safety management practice. This will cover the following aspects:

- assessment risk to participants
- measures identified as necessary to reduce risk; and
- arrangements to give continued effects to these measures.

The regulations themselves also make interesting reading since they are very carefully worded, as will become evident later in the chapter.

Implications of risk assessment legislation

Before leaving the subject of legislation, we should note the use of the phrase 'suitable and sufficient assessment'. The phrase is used in other regulations made under the 1974 Act and arguably has profound legal implications. What precisely is 'suitable' and how much is 'sufficient'? Reference to 'competent person' (to supervise customers, train staff, check equipment, carry out risk assessment procedures, etc.) is also becoming more frequent. The implication here is obvious – managers must ensure that they do the following:

- employ staff whose qualifications are valid in terms of the body/organization which issues those qualifications (lifeguarding qualifications, for example, have a finite duration)
- employ a sufficient number of competent staff to cover the activities being organized or supervised
- where risk is greatest, engage expert individuals or organizations to advise on, or carry out, risk assessment procedures.

The question arises 'Is experience sufficient to prove competence?'. In a society which is growing more litigious, there must be 'someone to blame' for any accident. That 'someone' is often a corporate body. Wishing to avoid liability wherever possible, managers look to institutions – such as national governing bodies of sport – to validate competence, even where there may be in-house training programmes. As a result, 'experience alone' is regrettably becoming less and less acceptable, in the leisure industry as elsewhere.

Risk assessment principles

Risk assessment can never be a precise science in the sense that accidents at a precise time in a precise place can be predicted. None the less, accident records do show a pattern which acts as a guide to the future.

For reasons explained above, managers would be well advised to seek external expert assistance whenever possible. By so doing, the manager is exercising a reasonable 'duty of care', and is also, in some cases, transferring some of the legal liability away from his or her own organization to a third party. Provided that third party is insured, it may become the 'deepest pocket' worth suing!

Having obtained an expert opinion, it would obviously be foolish to ignore that opinion. Consequently, the second guiding principle must be to minimize the risks identified – by adopting 'good practice' in all aspects of the operation.

Thirdly if some risks remain – which must be the case in 'fun' facilities such as fun-fairs, water parks, theme parks, as well as in certain sports – then the manager must ensure that the risk is limited to that which the customer may reasonably anticipate.

The situation with regard to youngsters is especially onerous, in that under-18s are regarded by the courts as being less able to identify – and therefore accept – the risks associated with an activity.

The fourth principle has become most important in cases of medical litigation, and is increasingly being quoted in the leisure sphere. To merely tell the customer that 'this activity is risky', whether verbally or in writing, is no longer adequate. Instead, management may have to explain the nature of the risk – possibly even expressed in percentage terms – if the court is to be satisfied that the customer has been properly advised.

Companies and groups specialising in 'adrenaline sports' like bungee-jumping, wing-walking and sky-diving, find it very difficult to meet this criterion, of course.

Where the customer is under-18, 'explaining the risk', in whatever degree of detail, is not acceptable. Rather, the youngster simply cannot be exposed to a risk which is unreasonable.

Calculating risk

On the assumption that the individual customer has had the risk explained or is otherwise expected to be able to appreciate the nature of the risk, then the manager's role is limited to 'containing' the risks to those anticipated. Take away all external risk, of course, and there's no fun. A balance has therefore to be struck. The risk itself may be seen as a function of three factors:

- probability (P)
- severity (S)
- frequency (F)

where each of the three has a scale 0 to 10, and by use of the formula $P \times S \times F$. An alternative formula for risk rating is $F \times (S + MPL + P)$, where MPL represents 'maximum possible loss' on a scale 1 to 50.

Formulae to calculate the risk, using the above, cannot be completely accurate, since they are so tentative. 'Probability' for example, has to be assumed on the basis of 'previous accidents', or more precisely the 'number of previous accidents per participant over a period of time'. Where age-specific information is available (as with football accidents referred to earlier) then probability is easier to calculate, assuming one knows the age range of the customers.

'Severity', in relation to the minimum possible damage caused by a given accident, is perhaps easier to calculate, from the greater severity (death) to the least severe (no injury expected)

The third factor, 'frequency' is likewise capable of being measured, where participation rates are to hand.

Risk control

Once the risk has been identified, it needs somehow to be 'managed', and a comprehensive risk control strategy devised. Stranks (1994) considers risk control as having four components, namely:

1   Risk avoidance – closing the feature, or replacing the material, or scrapping the equipment
2   Risk retention – the risk is retained, in the knowledge that cost penalties are outweighed by the benefit associated with the risk

3   Risk transfer – where the risk is transferred to an outside 'expert person' or
    organization, e.g. through taking out insurance, or seeking an expert opinion
4   Risk reduction – where data is collected and a strategy adopted to reduce those
    risks, either within specific sections or across the organization as a whole.

Particular areas of risk

Two areas of high risk are examined in this section, the first relating to unpredictable customers, namely children, and the second to an unpredictably environment, namely water. With the Lyme Bay tragedy, both sets of circumstances
coincide, with dire consequences.

Accidents at playgrounds

Children can be injured at many locations other than playgrounds, as the aforementioned statistics show. However, because playgrounds are provided and
managed by many leisure organizations – at hotels, theme parks, recreation
grounds, etc. – the legal aspects attached to the risk need to be addressed.

Research carried out in 1991/92 by the MORI organization and commissioned
by the Audit Commission showed 'safety in playgrounds' to be the most important concern of people when considering all the different kinds of outdoor local
authority recreational services.

Probably the most comprehensive information is provided by the National
Playing Fields Association (NPFA) which can be read in conjunction with the DTI
figures. The NPFA points out however that it tends to be the more serious injuries
which are reported, with the vast number of minor accidents unrecorded, except
perhaps when they are dealt with by the casualty department of a major hospital.

Causes of accidents

The type and percentage of playground accidents reported to the NPFA for 1995
are as follows:

* falls – 69 per cent
* entrapment – 15 per cent

- struck by item – 3 per cent
- other – 13 per cent.

The NPFA also confirmed that a significant number of the 'other' accidents were the result of entrapments, usually beneath roundabouts.

As one might expect, a significant number of accidents are associated with a fall onto a hard surface. The NPFA identified equipment which is commonly linked with such accidents, as follows:

- slides – 36 per cent
- climbing frames – 24 per cent
- swings – 19 per cent
- overhead horizontal ladders – 4 per cent
- other – 17 per cent.

Some methodology relating to playground accidents was examined in a comprehensive study by King and Ball (1989). The study examined standards which apply in certain other countries, such as Holland, Denmark, France, Italy, Australia, New Zealand, Canada and the United States, and compared these to those which exist in the United Kingdom. One of the study's more surprising conclusions, for example, was as follows:

> The commonly held notion that head injuries constitute the majority of serious playground injuries is found to be invalid. Long bone fractures are far more prevalent, by factors of between twenty and one hundred.

The report went on to say:

> Analysis of the international data on playground-related hospital attendances and admissions reveals a marked degree of similarity among industrialized countries. If one examines the types of playground equipment-related injuries resulting in hospital attendance, it is found that approximately 1% are attributable to skull fractures, and 7% concussion or intracranial injury. Long bone fractures account for from 23% to 44% of those attendances.

Whilst many leisure managers may be tempted to believe that the installation of impact-absorbing surfacing beneath play equipment will solve all the problems, this appears to be over-optimistic. The study points out that this approach offers only a partial solution, for the following reasons:

- the primary cause of most playground injuries, whether serious or trivial, is not a fall from equipment with subsequent head impact with the ground.
- the current generation of 'safety surfacing' is designed to lessen the severity of head injuries resulting from impact with the ground, and not the severity of long bone injuries which are far more prevalent.
- even in the case of head-first falls onto resilient surfaces, there is still a finite risk of head injury.

The study concluded that accidents at playgrounds in the UK commonly showed the following:

- the majority of playground accidents involve falls on the same level e.g. collisions, stumbling and tripping
- head injuries tend to be predominant among the youngest age group (0 to 4 years), probably because of their undeveloped motor skills and lack of awareness
- the majority of head injuries consist of superficial wounds such as cuts and bruises
- serious injuries which have been caused by falls from height generally involve the upper limbs and not the head
- many of the serious head injuries can be attributed to causes such as being hit by swing seats and collisions, and not just falls from height.

The position, therefore, is not as simple as it first appeared. Certainly, managers of such facilities are expected to ensure that all equipment in situ conforms to current standards, and likewise that any new installation is carried out in conformity with those separate standards which apply (British Standards exist for each, and European Standards are under consideration). Nor should any equipment be modified, by management, once it is installed.

Supervision also appears to be very important, and a lack of adult scrutiny – by the parents or the management – could be a significant factor in accident rates. Understandably enough, the very presence of 'safety surfacing' suggests to some parents that the child simply cannot hurt itself in the playground, whatever misuse occurs.

Accidents in water

Water represents a dangerous environment, by anyone's standards. Leisure managers who are responsible for indoor swimming pools, outdoor swimming

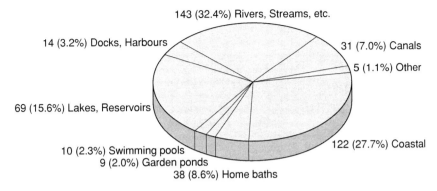

143 (32.4%) Rivers, Streams, etc.

14 (3.2%) Docks, Harbours

31 (7.0%) Canals

5 (1.1%) Other

69 (15.6%) Lakes, Reservoirs

122 (27.7%) Coastal

10 (2.3%) Swimming pools

9 (2.0%) Garden ponds

38 (8.6%) Home baths

Figure 7.9 Drowning in the UK, 1996, by location. Total number of drownings 441.
Source: RoSPA

pools, boating lakes, water parks, river banks and even paddling pools must be well aware of the risks which exist, particularly to children but also to adults.

Sometimes, it is not the water itself which brings about tragedy, but the equipment associated with it. When a water slide collapsed at a theme park (Waterworld USA) near San Francisco in June 1997, one girl died and 30 were injured, six critically. Apparently, the teenagers had tried to descend the slide in a 'human chain'. The glass-fibre half-pipe was simply unable to take the strain, and cracked halfway between supports, throwing some of the youngsters to a drop of 75 feet (*The Times*, 4 June 1997).

However, in order to put things into perspective, it is worth mentioning that this type of tragedy is very rare, and it may be thought that the unpredictable behaviour of the teenagers was a part-cause, though tolerance levels for the fibreglass pipe should have been calculated on the assumption that such a loading might conceivably occur.

Drownings are the ultimate accidents that happen in water. As mentioned earlier in the chapter, figures produced by RoSPA show that in 1996 drownings at swimming pools represented a very small proportion (2 per cent or 10 people) of the total. Of these 10 people, only one drowned at a public swimming pool, whereas five drowned at a home pool, and four at a private pool. A much higher number of drownings occurred in rivers and streams (32 per cent), coastal water (28 per cent) and lakes and reservoirs (16 per cent). Figure 7.9 shows the complete picture.

We can also see some correlation with age and with gender, where drownings are concerned. Male drownings outnumbered female drownings by 4 : 1, with the age

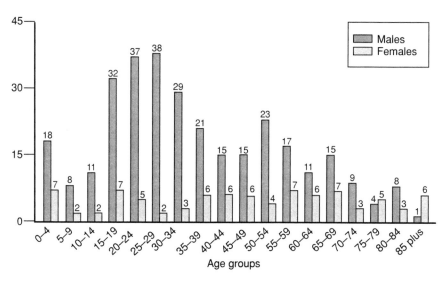

Figure 7.10   Drowning in the UK, 1996, by age group and sex. Male: 348, female: 92, gender unknown 1, ages unknown 42. *Source*: RoSPA

group most 'at risk' being 25–29 year olds, followed closely by 20–24 year olds, and then 15–19 year olds. Figure 7.10 also shows a high incidence of drownings for 0–4 year olds. Oddly, female drownings outnumber male drownings in only two age bands, namely 75–79, and 85+, and it would be interesting to know why this was so (gender longevity perhaps?) and in what circumstances the drownings occurred.

The tragedy of Lyme Bay

The Managing Director of an outdoor activity company (Active Learning and Leisure), Peter Kite, became the first company director to receive a prison sentence (three years initially, later reduced on appeal to two) for manslaughter. His co-defendant, Joseph Stoddart, who managed the Centre in Dorset at the time of the tragedy, was acquitted, after the jury failed to reach a majority verdict.

The relatively small 'span of control' and hierarchy (see Chapter 4) made the prosecution easier to sustain, since the accused could hardly claim they were totally unaware of key weaknesses in the operation of the Centre.

Previous attempts to prosecute companies in the criminal courts had stalled precisely on this issue, e.g. that brought against P&O Ferries in 1990 following the

Zeebrugge disaster. In this latter case, the concept of the 'company's mind' concerned the courts: the prosecution had to prove that events which brought about the accident were effectively part of company policy, as approved by the directors of that company. With Zeebrugge, the failures occurred at the lower end of the 'chain of command' and given the substantial 'span of control' the directors of P&O were absolved of blame.

Contributing factors

Let us briefly look at the failures and mistakes which culminated in the accident which occurred on 22 March 1993:

- on the day in question, the Southampton Weather Centre was predicting gusts of up to force five
- sea temperatures in late March are normally around 9°C (48°F)
- neither coastguard nor harbourmaster were advised that the expedition was about to take place
- the eight sixth-form students had received only half a day's instruction, at a swimming pool, before their expedition the very next day
- each of the two instructors had been on a basic course for three days during the previous week, and were inadequately qualified for sea canoeing
- no one carried distress flares
- the safety boat, which normally kept an eye on sea expeditions, was engaged elsewhere
- lifejackets were worn, but were only partially inflated.

The conditions were so treacherous that disaster quickly struck. One of the survivors, Emma Hartley (then 16) described what happened, in a statement read to the court. She told how members of the group ran into difficulties soon after leaving the beach at Lyme Regis at about 10 a.m. The youngsters were forced to link their canoes together, whilst waiting for their teacher, who had capsized on several occasions. Several of the youngsters' canoes also capsized and some lost their paddles. One by one, all the canoes filled with water, and the entire group was left clinging to an upturned canoe by about 11.30 a.m.

At 3.05 p.m., when the party was three hours overdue, Mr Stoddart alerted the coastguards, after spending some time driving along the shore to see if anything was amiss. Yet more time elapsed, while a shore-based search took place by coastguard officials. At 3.56 p.m. the first helicopter was called in, followed 30 minutes later by the Lyme Regis lifeboat. At 5.00 p.m. two more helicopters scrambled. At this point, only two people (one instructor and the teacher) were in their canoes, rafted together. They were finally rescued at 5.30 p.m. By the time the others were rescued, they had been in the water for almost three and a half hours, and by then four pupils, Simon Dunne, Claire Langley, Rachael Walker and Dean Sayer, were virtually unconscious. All four died. (*Daily Telegraph* and *Guardian*, November 1994).

The lessons of Lyme Bay

What lessons are to be learned from this terrible event? Clearly, it was the 'aggregation' of otherwise small failures which led to the tragedy: had the weather been better, the sea temperature warmer, the coastguard alerted sooner, etc. then the four youngsters might not have died.

The Centre's management had, after all, been warned – and herein lies a fundamental point. Anyone responsible for a leisure facility must exercise a duty of care towards those who visit that facility. Once the manager is advised that a danger exists – whether the warning comes from a member of the public or a member of staff – it is vital that the danger be removed.

Amazingly, the Centre had done nothing after being alerted that safety standards were inadequate. Two instructors, in letters of resignation sent in the June previous to the March accident, had said prophetically (*Guardian*, 13 May 1993):

> We think you should have a very early look at your standards of safety or else you could find yourself having to explain why someone's son or daughter will not be coming home ... there is most definitely not one person here technically qualified to instruct ... we are walking a very fine line between getting away with it and having a very serious accident.

In other words, the Centre had been advised that standards of safety were inadequate. Having done nothing to rectify these inadequacies, the management of the Centre put itself in a totally vulnerable position, when faced with distraught parents, traumatized survivors, and eventually proceedings at Winchester Crown Court.

The implications of Lyme Bay

Whilst at the time of the accident there was no formal licensing procedure, the general principles of risk assessment, health and safety rules and duty of care placed legal responsibilities on the shoulders of the company and its Director. All those who organize – or subcontract – leisure events must have regard to this extreme case. The 'what if?' approach can receive no better testimony than the Lyme Regis accident. What if this was your Centre? What if this was your child?

The following points should be borne in mind:

1   The Health and Safety at Work etc. Act 1974 specifies that employers must establish safe systems of work. The company had palpably failed to provide safe systems to protect either their own staff or their young clients.
2   The 'duty of care' principle would imply that staff responsible for the young-sters should be properly qualified for that task. Ironically, the British Canoe Union (BCU) had been pressing the Government to make it compulsory for activity centre instructors to hold full qualifications – whereas the two instruc-tors at Lyme Regis held only one-star awards, the most basic type of BCU certificate.
3   The fact that children were involved makes it even more important that due attention be paid to their safety, in accordance with the terms of the Occupiers' Liability Act 1957. It could not be argued, by way of defence, that the young-sters 'knew the risks and were therefore partly responsible for what happened'.

The tragedy at Craven Arms

'Failing to ensure safety under the Health and Safety at Work etc. Act' was also the charge levied at another adventure centre, this time at Craven Arms, Shrop-shire, in 1993. An 11-year-old girl, Hayley Hadfield, died after an unqualified instructor was allowed to take 30 children on what magistrates described as a 'stupid' short cut during a cross-country hike. The youngster suffered fatal head injuries after falling down a steep slope and hitting a tree. No help was raised until one hour after the accident, and emergency procedures were described as 'lamentable' (*Daily Telegraph*, 10 November 1993).

The firm in this case, Globerow Ltd, was fined £15 000 and ordered to pay costs. Its Managing Director, Vaughan Philips, was also fined £15 000. In the light of what happened in the Lyme Regis case, it may be considered surprising that more serious charges were not similarly brought.

Licensing of outdoor activity centres in the United Kingdom

Immediately after the Lyme Bay tragedy there were vociferous calls for mandatory licensing. Prior to the accident, a voluntary code was being drawn up by various interested parties (represented by the British Activity Holiday Association) and was published in 1994. A private Members' Bill to make licensing statutory, rather than voluntary, was initially promulgated by the Labour MP for Plymouth, David Jamieson, from whose constituency the four teenagers came. The proposal received cross-party support, as well as the backing of the Schools Minister, Eric Forth. It was duly redrafted in the form of a government Bill, and thereafter became an Act of Parliament.

In the meantime, and prior to establishing the licensing authority, the government issued Circular Number 22/94 ('Safety in Outdoor Activity Centres: Guidance) in September 1994. Although superseded in part by subsequent regulations, the circular is still invaluable to those who may be contemplating taking youngsters to such a centre.

The Activity Centres (Young Persons' Safety) Act 1995

The Act is introduced as follows:

> An Act to make provision for the regulation of centres and providers of facilities whose children and young persons under the age of 18 engage in adventure activities, including provision for the imposition of requirements relating to safety.

The Act effectively established the licensing regime (Para I [1]), and paved the way for the regulations which were to follow in 1996 (Para 3 [1]). It also confirmed what 'fell outside' the new rules, namely:

1   facilities which are provided exclusively for persons who have attained the age of 18, or
2   facilities which do not consist of, or include some element of, instruction or leadership'. (Para 1 [3.a.b])

Finally, the Act makes it an offence:

1   to do anything for which a licence is required under the regulations, otherwise than in accordance with the licence, or

2   for the purposes of obtaining a licence –
    i   to make a statement to the licensing authority (or someone acting on their behalf) knowing it to be false in a manner particular, or
    ii recklessly to make a statement to the licensing authority (or someone acting on their behalf) which is false in a material particular.

Essentially, (i) above refers to a deliberate lie whereas (ii) refers to an action which is tantamount to a lie, being a 'reckless' action in itself.

The Adventure Activities Licensing Regulations 1996

The Order establishing the regulations came into force in April 1996.

As has been mentioned in another context, these particular regulations mark something of a departure: their stringency, and the degree of control to be exercised by the licensing authority, makes the regulations tighter even than many which relate to the workplace.

Risk assessment is an integral part of these regulations. And the 'Interpretation' section (5[I]) is so carefully constructed that one must give credit to such thoroughness. The wording is as follows:

> The licensing authority may grant or refuse a licence, but without prejudice to its discretion to refuse a licence on other grounds, the authority shall not grant a licence unless ... it is satisfied that the applicant has –
>   i   made a suitable and sufficient assessment of the risks to the safety of the young persons and other persons who will be involved in the adventure activities in respect of which the application is made or whose safety may be affected thereby;
>   ii identified the measures he needs to take in consequence of that assessment to ensure, so far as is reasonably acceptable, the safety of those persons ...
>   iii appointed competent persons to advise him on safety matters or has competence in such matters himself.

The point worth noting is that related to the 'Conditions', which are quite specific, as follows (Para 7 [I:b]):

> the licence holder shall maintain suitable and sufficient arrangements –
>   i   for the appointment of a sufficient number of competent and adequately qualified instructors;
>   ii for the giving of safety information to instructors and participants;

iii for the provision of such equipment as is needed to ensure that the activities are carried out safely;

iv for the maintenance of that equipment in an efficient state and in good repair;

v for the provision of first-aid, for the summoning of medical and rescue services in the event of an emergency, and for otherwise dealing with an emergency.

Conclusions

On all counts, one can sense the terrible echoes of the Lyme Bay accident in the carefully crafted words of subsequent legislation.

Some three years after the Lyme Bay tragedy, and as a result of various accidents in the Cairngorms, there was a call to regulate mountaineering, through compulsory insurance and minimum qualifications. A remarkable 460 per cent increase in mountaineering accidents in 30 years was not the only explanation for the problem, and the general secretary of the British Mountaineering Council pointed out that there had been an increased participation of 494 per cent during the same period.

The president of the international mountaineering organization was reported to have said (*Guardian*, 2 December 1995).

> One of the falsehoods is that if you obey the rules then you will be all right. In many ways, having rules de-sensitises people to the risks. There really are no hard and fast rules that can protect you. It's all about taking risks – if you remove the risk then there isn't a sport.

This in many ways is the nub of the matter. If all risk is removed from leisure, including sport, then what remains? My own view is that rules do not, in fact, 'de-sensitise people to the risks' but on the contrary emphasize that risks are present. The wider argument, about risk removal, is more complicated because what may be acceptable in one era, or state, may not be acceptable in other. The very pervasive 'culture of blame' and the tendency of injured parties to take legal action, has undoubtedly made the general public more aware of their rights, in relation to risk exposure.

The leisure manager's job has changed as a result of the same forces, and no longer is it satisfactory to leave risk-assessment training out of the frame.

One hopes that readers – whether future or current managers – will sense how important a topic the author feels risk assessment to be. Risks in relation to leisure vary in their quality and quantity, according to the activity and venue – but should never be ignored.

The sombre lesson to be derived from accidents referred to within the text is not increased or diminished by the scale of each one. Events at Craven Arms, Lyme Bay, Isle of Man, Bradford and Hillsborough were terrible in that with the benefit of hindsight none need have happened.

If this brief mention serves to prevent even one accident in the future, then it can have no greater tribute.

Risk assessment is being demanded more and more often and not only at outdoor activity centres. Theatres are also growing more concerned with risk assessment and safety issues, with the National Entertainment Safety Association (NESA) collaborating with Theatrical Technical Training Services to provide a database of information about United Kingdom and EU health and safety standards (*The Stage*, 12 June 1997).

References and recommended reading

Audit Commission. (1994). *Leisure Services Playgrounds and Play Areas*.

Bannister, J.E. and Bawcutt, I.A. (1981). *Practical Risk Management*. Witherby and Co. (Chapter IV on the subject of risk control is especially relevant.)

Health and Safety Executive. (1989). *Human Factors in Industrial Safety*. HMSO, London.

Health and Safety Executive. (1989). *Quantified Risk Assessment: Its Impact & Decision Making*. HMSO, London.

Health and Safety Executive. (1991). *Successful Health and Safety Management*. HMSO, London.

King, K. and Ball, D. (1989). *A Holistic Approach to Accident and Injury Prevention in Children's Playgrounds*. (Published originally by a division of Rendel Scientific Services Ltd.) Copies obtainable from: D.J. Ball, 3 Anchor Quay, Norwich NR3 3PR, Tel/fax: 01603 665422, E-Mail: david.ball@paston.co.uk

RoSPA (1995). *Children's Playgrounds in Small Communities*. Sponsored by Wickstead Leisure.

Society of Public Health. (1990). *Do We Pay Too Much for Our Sport and Leisure Activities?*

Sports Council/Health and Safety Commission. (1987). *Safety in Swimming Pools*. Sports Council with Health and Safety Commission.

Stranks, J. (1994). *Management Systems for Safety*. Pitman Publishing.

Summerland Fire Commission. (1974). *Report*. Government Office, Isle of Man.

Which? (1994). *Danger in the Playground*. July.

8 The leisure manager's role

Questions

At the end of this chapter you should be able to undertake the following:

1 Consider whether leisure managers should receive 'once-only' training, at degree or HND level, or whether some other form of training would be preferable.
2 Discuss the argument that a leisure manager should be trying to improve the quality of life, and not merely meeting demand.
3 Indicate the documentation which a newly appointed leisure manager might usefully peruse, in relation to the management of staff, of money and of physical resources.

Introduction

The final chapter tries to peer forward, just a little, from what has gone before. After all, those who purport to be qualified in leisure management will be expected by potential employers to understand a good deal of the practice, as well as all of the theory.

As we have seen, a great deal of the theory is common to other disciplines. For example, a knowledge of finance is expected of virtually all managers nowadays, and risk management is taken as a fine art in the air traffic business. Event management is largely a matter of common sense, albeit assisted by some years of experience. And then there is the law: very little is unique to the leisure industry per se, only in the licensing of larger stadia and of certain outdoor activity centres.

The reader may legitimately ask 'So what's the big deal? Why is there a need to train people in leisure management? Can in fact leisure managers be trained, given the diversity of venues, resources, programmes and events?'

The answers are perhaps implicit within the chapters of this book: in brief they are as follows:

- Though much of the knowledge (within leisure management) is common to other professions, the judgement as to 'what applies' and 'how it applies' is often remarkably complex.
- The public actually does expect managers to be trained, whatever may sometimes be claimed, though it may not necessarily distinguish between training-through-study and training-through-experience.
- The legal, social and moral contexts are such that to have an untrained manager would be asking for trouble. Since litigation now follows so swiftly upon accident, a manager must create situations which are as safe as possible or as 'fully explained' as possible.
- The sheer size of the industry and the expectations which it generates – with the exception of home-based leisure – combine to create a new quantity (and quality) of risk, not seen previously.

One hopes that these arguments will convince any reader who has remained sceptical throughout the book. Any job, after all, looks far simpler to an outsider than to the person who undertakes it. Should more justification be needed, the sceptic may wish to read on; to those who wish to prepare for a leisure management job, or even an interview, the elaboration which follows may be of assistance, moving as it does firmly into the realm of 'practice'.

The aspects chosen are also useful in that they illustrate some of the points made in the text, which may here be summarized as follows:

- Conversance – the manager must be conversant with the physical resources for which he or she is legally responsible.
- Inspiration – the manager must be able to inspire the staff, while bearing in mind that organizational objectives must be fulfilled.
- Application – the manager must be able to convince others that he or she has the necessary knowledge and enthusiasm to undertake the task in hand.
- Vigilance – the manager must ensure that he or she knows the rules and regulations, all the while protecting the well-being of staff, customers and contractors.

We go on to look at five distinct management roles, as follows:

1   Managing fitness centres
2   Managing watersports
3   Managing spectator venues
4   Managing children's activities
5   Managing leisure land.

Some other roles have been considered separately, e.g. the promotion of programmes and events (Chapter 6) and the management of activity centres (Chapter 7). A brief section on job prospects concludes the chapter.

Managing fitness centres

Fitness centres are really 'Model 1' facilities on our scale (see Chapter 7), with a predictable environment (rooms, lighting, temperature controls, fixed equipment, but perhaps some free weights), being used by trained customers. Often the management task is to increase the diversity or challenge which is available to the customer, by introducing new equipment or new regimes.

The growth in fitness centres to some extent reflects the demands of those who are money-rich but time-poor, rather as squash clubs developed a certain cache and clientele during the boom years of the 1970s and 1980s.

Fitness machinery itself is relatively straightforward, with different items available for upper body/lower body/cardio-vascular exercise. For the most part, a manager's role in such an environment is about sustaining interest, often through social aspects attached to club membership and through the introduction of personalized fitness programmes.

Customers have clear expectations of the experience they are likely to undergo and there is very little environmental risk as such. Notwithstanding, there are aspects of fitness centre management which are quite distinct, and they are mentioned because they reinforce what has been said about the interface between the environment and the customer.

Fitness equipment

• Fitness equipment should be selected carefully. A huge choice is available, some more robust than others. The 'multi-unit' approach has generally been replaced by individual units for upper and lower body, and for cardio-vascular exercise. Purchasers are advised to check around for quality and 'value for money' (new equipment is very expensive, and depreciation substantial).

- Fitness equipment should also be purchased with parts-availability and maintenance in mind: the more robust the machinery the less the wear-and-tear. Manufacturers and/or suppliers guarantees should be sought.
- Fitness equipment should conform to an approved standard: since much of it is manufactured in the United States (and sold under licence) the standards of materials and construction are generally high.
- The equipment should be used in strict accordance with the manufacturers' instructions. Modification, by the centre's management, should never be contemplated for reasons of product liability (see Chapter 2).

Customers

- Customers should be carefully screened – again for legal reasons – with as much responsibility laid upon them for assessing their own fitness as possible. Initial checks by the centre are recommended, however, e.g. for blood pressure and heart-rate at exercise levels.
- Customers should therefore be recommended (in writing) to see their General Practitioners if they have any doubts as to their physical condition or the suitability of the exercise being contemplated.
- Induction sessions should be carried out, once the screening process is complete. These should be designed to make the customer feel confident about using each item of equipment, with any possible hazards pointed out.
- Customers using free weights in the same space as fixed fitness equipment should receive specific instructions as to their use.
- Whilst the centre is in operation, visual scanning (possibly by CCTV) is essential in case of equipment misuse or emergency.

Provided that these simple precautions are followed, the fitness centre should operate well, so long as it offers the right service for the right price.

One point remains however, and that relates to the initial screening process. This is done in part by some basic tests but additionally some lifestyle questions may be put in the form of a questionnaire. However tempting it might appear, the presence of too many questions may place the interviewer, i.e. the fitness centre manager, in an extremely invidious position. The author recalls one newly appointed manager who devised a six-page questionnaire which asked very specific medical questions (her husband was a doctor) such as 'have you ever been diagnosed as having any respiratory problem?' While her enthusiasm was laudable, the questions – or rather the answers – raised a host of problems, notably because the centre had to decide how then to act upon the knowledge provided by the respondent.

Where it is reasonable not to know everything which can be known about a customer's medical condition – as was surely the case here – then better not to ask in the first place. As ever, the manager must decide what is reasonable in the circumstances, and given the liability attached to the activity would be wise to seek advice from a trade association or lawyer before proceeding unilaterally.

Managing watersports

Water is a very special resource since its usage for leisure purposes can be so wonderful yet so very problematical. Its inherent characteristics make watersports especially risky, moreso where untrained individuals are tempted to 'take to the water'. Chapter 7 examined one particular tragedy, that of Lyme Bay, but in a sense each lifeboat-rescue is a near-accident, rather like a near-miss in air traffic terms. The resource itself is found in several forms:

- sea-water (tidal/non-tidal, seas, estuaries)
- fresh water (rivers, lakes, ponds, canals).

In both cases, there are management responsibilities attached to the points at which the land meets the water. This may seem obvious enough, but coastal zone management, riparian ownership and even towpath management present distinct challenges, moreso where the site is public open space. Though the site is technically 'land', in the previous definition, none the less there are especial risks simply because of its proximity to water. The same argument applies to the management of open air swimming pools, of course.

Equally, the management of people-on-the-water is fraught with potential problems because of the coincidence between an unpredictable environment (such as the sea) and, all too often, an untrained (and therefore unpredictable) individual.

Sea currents and winds can quickly separate whole parties, and 'creating a bolt-hole' if the weather turns nasty, as in the mountains, is not an option.

Managers who have some responsibility for the water/land mixture rather than for watersports activities alone, are expected to give consideration to the following:

- Ownership – who owns the land immediately adjacent to the water, in the case of rivers, ponds, lakes.
- Access – whether the public has any right of access onto that land, e.g. a public footpath along a river bank.
- Usage – whether another organization has rights to enter into the area, in order to use the water, e.g. fishing club, sub-aqua club, canoe club.
- Risks – whether there are any particular risks associated with the site, irrespective of whether or not public access is a legal right, e.g. a river bank which has been undermined by strong currents.

Watersports management may coincidentally involve the above-mentioned issues, but in addition carries the substantial responsibility for public safety. The following guidance should therefore be considered:

- Legal compliance – ensuring strict compliance to the guidelines or rules issued by respective governing bodies of sport (in the case of the United Kingdom) or by any other competent authorities
- Equipment – providing equipment that is thoroughly checked, and of a specification appropriate to the circumstances of use
- Instructors – checking that instructors are fully qualified to undertake the roles expected of them
- Checks – where sea/estuary usage is concerned, ensuring that checks are made as to tides, weather forecasts and wind conditions
- Procedures – ensuring that emergency procedures are known to all personnel, and that adherence is absolute
- Risk assessment – ensuring that risk assessment is carried out when required by law (see Chapter 7 with regard to the aftermath of Lyme Bay).

Where buildings are involved, and particularly where residential accommodation is made available, the following guidelines should also be observed:

- Standards – checking that fixtures, fittings, plant and equipment are provided and maintained in accordance with approved standards, where applicable
- Licences – ensuring that all conditions attached to licences are adhered to, and that any additional licences are sought when necessary (see Chapter 2)
- Fire regulations – ensuring that the building is used in accordance with fire regulations, where applicable, and that nothing is done that might jeopardize either emergency egress by the public or emergency access by fire or ambulance services
- Building regulations – where applicable, checking that any modifications being considered are in accordance with the regulations

- Planning consent – ensuring that the usage of the building is in accordance with the planning consent and with any special conditions attached thereto
- Insurance – providing insurance cover, as appropriate to particular events, and ensuring cover for 'public liability' and for staff
- Insurance – ensuring that nothing is done (or not done) that might jeopardize the provision of insurance cover.

Chapter 7 describes in some detail the errors which though perhaps small in themselves accumulated to create the terrible loss of life at Lyme Bay. This must be an object lesson to those who offer watersports as part of any outdoor activity programme, if such accidents are not to be repeated.

But what of adults? How is a watersports manager to react if an adult customer claims to be experienced at wind-surfing or sea canoeing? Trickier still, what if the adult brings his or her own equipment along?

As we have seen in Chapter 2 the principle is that adults must take some responsibility for their own actions, and cannot always be protected from themselves. However, in such circumstances and given the unpredictability of a maritime environment, the watersports manager would be recommended to observe the customer starting the activity in the first place, and to check the customer's equipment beforehand. Should doubts remain, the customer may be asked to sign a document confirming that he or she was briefed on the risks as well as on the deficiencies in his or her equipment but none the less wished to proceed.

Managing spectator venues

Chapter 7 referred to a situation where the leisure environment is an aggregate of customers. Under certain circumstances, such as the outbreak of fire or a fight, the crowd may constitute a sizeable and unpredictable hazard. Crowd psychology then develops its own momentum, almost irrespective of the original cause – particularly when the cause itself (as at Bradford) is actually visible.

The responsibilities attached to the management of large entertainment and sporting venues should never be underestimated therefore. Football stadia in particular – and rugby stadia to a lesser extent – pose problems of crowd management which are quite distinct, and quite unlike most other managerial roles. In such circumstances, the following aspects are considered important:

- Structures – ensuring that the physical fabric of the stadium/theatre/concert hall is in a sound structural condition
- Systems – ensuring that all sound, lighting, emergency lighting systems are in working order
- Fire detection – ensuring that detection systems and appliances are working properly, so that once a fire breaks out, alarms are activated as appropriate
- Fire fighting – ensuring that all component parts of the fire-fighting system are in good order, namely:

  hose reels: usually fixed along escape routes or close to fire exits

  'dry risers': an empty pipe rising vertically inside a building, with an inlet provided at ground level to allow the fire service to pump water into the riser from the nearest hydrant

  'wet risers': a permanent connection to a water supply capable of providing the necessary pressure at the top outlet

  sprinklers: pipes usually fixed at ceiling level throughout the protected area. Sprinkler heads are connected to the pipes and, in the event of a fire, the heat causes a flexible element in the nearest sprinkler head to shatter and allows water to be discharged in the form of a spray.
- Training – ensuring that all internal staff (stewards, front of house, stage staff, bar/catering staff, etc.) are fully trained in emergency procedures. (Deficiencies in evacuation procedures were noted as highly significant in the Summerland disaster, referred to in Chapter 7)
- Security – ensuring that external services (police, fire, ambulance) are fully integrated into the operation as a whole, and are given the opportunity to review procedures as well as monitor operations (Twickenham serves as a good example of this process)
- Licensing – ensuring that all conditions attached to the licence are met in full
- Monitoring and control – ensuring that 'pressure points' outside or inside the ground/venue do not build up to the point where they could conceivably have a major effect (as at Hillsborough). CCTV is now used extensively to scan a facility in its entirety.

Even with all these precautions and all these systems, the possibility of a serious accident can never be ruled out. When upwards of 75 000 people attend a football or rugby match there is always the risk of a minor incident becoming a major disaster.

The management role in such an environment is dominated by considerations of public safety, whether the venue is a stadium (largely uncovered) or an arena (covered). Controlling and monitoring large numbers of people requires systems that are tried and tested – plus regular liaison with emergency services. The structures themselves, especially at older venues, should be checked regularly to ensure that nothing is amiss. Roof canopies in particular need to be checked for the effects of weathering.

Above all, there must be operating procedures ('normal' and 'emergency') which are clearly defined, communicated to all personnel and practised on a regular basis.

Any 'conditions of hire' must also be carefully worded, due to the quality and quantity of the liability being transferred to the external hirer. One is often surprised to see such documentation being used year after year – though the legal environment has changed almost beyond recognition.

Any long-term lease, e.g. to a football club, must also be constructed in such a way as to make clear the respective responsibilities of the lessor (the organization granting the lease) and the lessee (the organization taking the lease). Again, the former would be well advised to check that the documentation provides adequate safeguards in the event of an accident.

Managing children's activities

So many private sector, public authorities and local organizations provide activities for children that the topic justifies some attention in a text such as this. Often, these activities are promulgated in the form of complete programmes ('summer holiday playschemes' or 'Easter camps'), but more rarely in the form of single-activity workshops, e.g. for visual art or drama. Often sporting activity is predominant, as with outdoor programmes presented in parks and open spaces.

An important distinction lies between residential and non-residential programmes. One hopes that enough has been said in the text to indicate why this distinction is so crucial, but for the avoidance of doubt some points are made here. (It should also be borne in mind that outdoor activity centres fall into the former ambit, and as such are close in character to the camp-based programmes offered by other organizations.)

Residential programmes for children are especially popular in the United States, the best-known company being Camp America. Whereas there is an accepted tradition of 'going off to camp' in the United States, the situation in the United Kingdom is rather different. Jackson (1997) suggests that, unlike their American counterparts, British parents feel guilty about 'sending their children away' in the first place! Be that as it may, the growth of companies such as PGL Holidays, Camp Beaumont, and Superchoice indicates that the American tradition may become popular elsewhere – provided of course that no disasters occur.

Having regard to what has been said about risk management in Chapter 7, what can we say to advise the manager who is responsible for such programmes?

The topic as a whole can be considered in terms of the following:

- provision of physical facilities
- staff selection, training and development
- provision of equipment
- provision of support services (transport, etc.)
- provision of subcontracted services.

In addition, where residential accommodation is provided, there will be:

- provision of sleeping/social accommodation.

Clearly, there is a much greater responsibility falling upon management when the youngster is present on site for 24 hours per day. In that instance the legal liability of ensuring the child's safety remains throughout the whole period. With non-residential programmes, the liability exists from the point of hand-over, by the parent, to the point of collection. (In one's experience, difficulties are caused when the child is allowed to leave a site unaccompanied, having been told by his or her parents to 'make your own way home'.)

In brief, one might usefully examine each of the foregoing.

Provision of physical facilities

Programme organizers should satisfy themselves, by a prior site inspection, that the site is safe and secure (from intruders or unauthorized egress). Any dangerous item within the site may conceivably be seen as an 'allurement' by the courts, should an accident occur, e.g. an open-air swimming pool within a school compound. Buildings too must be secure, and any dangerous areas made physically inaccessible. Checks must be made to ensure that there is the physical means to raise an alarm (i.e. by telephone or radio) should an accident occur.

Staff selection, training and development

Given the vulnerability of the customers, every precaution must be taken to protect their physical and psychological well-being. Staff selection procedures should be discussed with the police (with regard to possible screening process) and ideally with a legal expert, lest future problems arise. Any staff employed to undertake sports coaching should have the appropriate qualifications, for which proof should be provided. Staff training should be compulsory, and should include emergency procedures as well as normal operating procedures. Staff deployment should be consistent with their qualifications, notably where sporting activities are provided.

Provision of equipment

Equipment must be purchased well in advance of the programme's commencement, and should be checked as to its specification (in the case of sports equipment). High-risk sports, such as trampolining, and gymnastics should not be contemplated unless thorough checks have been made.

Provision of support services

Provision of support services, e.g. for food and transport, should also be checked carefully. Coach operators must comply with certain rules, as must those who sell unwrapped food. (In this last regard, advice should be sought as to precautions in cooking outdoors, for instance.)

Provision of subcontracted services

The subcontracting of activities can be fraught with problems, even if at first sight the principle appears simple enough.

Due to economies of scale, subcontracting may take place in such matters as transport (see above), but also for high-risk and medium-risk activities, notably horse-riding, quad-bike riding, mountain biking and canoeing.

Any subcontractor should be carefully vetted: some will need to be licensed (e.g. horse-riding establishments), and all will need their own insurance for public liability. Neither form of documentation should be assumed, but personally checked and recorded.

Provision of sleeping/social accommodation

Two words should enter the mind of the reader, namely 'safety' and 'control' since both are respectively entailed by the two types of accommodation being provided. Risks attached to the provision of sleeping accommodation are particularly onerous, and all systems (for smoke detection, alarms, emergency lighting) must be thoroughly and regularly checked, as must all installations (fire doors, in situ fire-fighting items). In addition, staff must be trained in emergency procedures, and their training sessions duly recorded.

Provision of supervision and monitoring

To an extent, this is a 'catch-all' phrase, intended to represent what is generally expected of someone who manages activities for children. There may for example be minimum levels of supervision, as laid down in an Act of Parliament, or there may be higher standards which the organization itself – or the chosen venue – expects to see in operation.

On a general point, it may be assumed that managing activities for children is itself 'child's play'. One hopes that the foregoing will convince the reader that this is assuredly not the case ...

Managing leisure land

Like any other physical resource, land must be managed so as to retain its asset value. Managing public open space is especially problematical, however, given the conflicts of recreational usage (e.g. between different conservation groups) which inevitably occur.

Managing privately owned land which is used primarily for leisure purposes is altogether more straightforward a task, since access may be limited to organized clubs and societies.

Whether the land is used as a golf course, football pitch, allotment, nature reserve or whatever, the following aspects need to be addressed by any person about to assume that responsibility.

- Land tenure – whether the site is freehold or leasehold
- Land extent – the precise boundary curtilage should be known, e.g. for the reason of liability
- Land status – whether the land is public open space, common land, Crown land, private land
- Land restrictions – whether there are any restrictions on the uses to which the land may be put, e.g. planning restrictions, restrictive covenants, conservation designations (such as SSSI)

- Access – whether the public has a legal right of access onto the land, e.g. access agreements, statutory footpaths, bridleways
- Access – whether any other organization or agency has any rights of access over the land, e.g. easements to electricity companies to maintain overhead cables
- Land quality – whether the land has a particular environmental quality (protected or not) which creates its leisure interest, in which case a specific management regime will be required, e.g. to maintain heather moorland or wild flower meadows
- Land quality – whether below-ground conditions are such as to affect existing usage or restrict future usage, e.g. former land-fill sites, where methane emission may create immediate problems and also inhibit construction works
- Land location – whether any problems have occurred as a result of the site's location, e.g. from flooding or from air-borne pollution.

Clearly, while the above-mentioned aspects are relevant, they represent only the initial steps in the land management process. As often as not, land used for leisure purposes is, in the United Kingdom at least, designated public open space, and therefore has a measure of protection. In essence, local authorities cannot dispose of such assets, except under very special circumstances.

Managers of any land to which the public has open access (common, public open space, village greens, play areas) should ensure their familiarity with the legal states of their sites, and of any rules for governance ('by-laws') attached thereto.

Managers of private land, to which the public has no automatic right of access, should ensure that adequate contracts and checks are in place to protect public safety and the quality of the land itself.

Both types of manager would be wise to acquaint themselves with the detail of the legislation on occupiers' liability (see Chapter 2), and possibly on rights of way (if appropriate).

Jobs within the leisure industry

Preparing to work within such a diverse industry cannot be an easy matter, however many leisure management courses are created. To make things worse, courses are sometimes taught by individuals who have had no management experience whatever, but only know the theory. Whether this book helps to redress the balance is for the reader to decide, but in the meantime some suggestions are offered to students who are about to embark on a course (notwithstanding the criticism above) or upon the hunt for a real job.

- Check the job advert carefully: does it specify a qualification or minimum years of experience? If so, are you likely to be interviewed, i.e. do you meet the specification?
- Is your Curriculum Vitae (CV) suitable for this particular application? Does the employer ask for a CV in any case?
- Having received the Job Details or Personal Specification (howsoever titled), devise a CV or a covering letter which follows the same pattern, e.g. in referring to knowledge or skills.
- Play on your strengths, and identify knowledge and experience gained from part-time/casual employment as well as from full-time work.
- Even where previous full-time jobs may not seem relevant, consider whether in fact there is some connection that you could use, e.g. knowledge of building construction could be extremely useful in some leisure management roles, as would retail or marketing experience in others.
- Consider what additional knowledge would give you an advantage: this is especially true of health and safety legislation (and procedures), financial principles and practices and legal aspects generally.

Before committing oneself to a course, one should be aware of the desired 'end-result' in terms of job sought. For example, anyone wishing to concentrate on open space management may be wiser to undertake a postgraduate course in the discipline. Equally, anyone wishing to carry out open space maintenance would need to have a qualification in horticulture and possibly in arboriculture.

Working in the arts is more dependent upon simple flair, fortune and particular skills, e.g. design, promotion, marketing, finance and so forth, than on any single 'vocational qualification'. However, museum work is quite distinct, since its curators are drawn mostly from graduates in history or archaeology, just as art gallery staff are generally graduates in the visual arts.

Sports management too has become an all-graduate/HND profession. In addition, coaching qualifications are useful to obtain that 'first job', which is also true of sports development work. A knowledge of the law, as it relates to leisure services, has also become necessary.

Leisure management courses should certainly provide a useful stepping stone – either to a further (more specialized) short course, or to a longer postgraduate course, or to a temporary job or to a permanent job.

Conclusions

The four watchwords referred to earlier – conversance, inspiration, application and vigilance – should serve as guidelines for those about to enter this exciting industry. Though 'fun' and 'enjoyment' are perhaps uppermost in the minds of customers, managers should always bear in mind that leisure can be a 'deadly business'. Furthermore, potential managers need to recognize that major liabilities will be attached to the post which they will eventually hold.

But there remain enormous opportunities for satisfaction, despite the slings and arrows which will inevitably come the manager's way. The 'fingertips approach' – knowing a little, assuming everything will work out – is no longer an adequate option. Better to have a firm grasp on reality and to know what may go wrong.

Whether the leisure manager does indeed improve the 'quality of life' (of the customers) depends on the values that are ascribed to the particular service. Merely to occupy the time of youngsters, say, by managing an amusement arcade can hardly be seen as socially beneficial, whereas the provision of a summer sports programme can create a life-long pattern of activity.

Ultimately, managers have to justify the job to themselves, since not all leisure management roles may have social objectives – some may even have anti-social ones.

The author's view is that leisure is like so many other assets – you get out of it what you put into it. Implicit in this hypothesis is the notion that effort is required to make the best of life. One hopes that this book will have helped to make the point.

References and recommended reading

Central Council of Physical Recreation. (1994). *Governing Body Qualifications in Outdoor Pursuits and Water Recreation.*

Fitness for Industry. (1996). *Career Opportunities.*

Fyfe, L. (1994). *Careers in Sport.* Kogan Page.

Hobsons. (1994). *Handbook of Tourism and Leisure.*

Jackson, D. (1997). *Quad biking was brill; abseiling was brill, The Independent,* 7 June.

Sports Council. (1994). *Training and Education Courses.*

Torkildsen, G. (1995). *Leisure and Recreation Management.* E. & F.N. Spon.

Trotman. (1995). *Careers in Sport.* Trotman & Co. Ltd.

Index